Praise for *Dancing Mindfulness:*
A Creative Path to Healing and Transformation

"Jamie's work … strike[s] a chord. She has unique appeal among the very people who need her work most.… A welcome force among the members of Dance First, supporting the mission of 'movement before medication.'"

—Mark Metz, founder, Dance First Association;
publisher, *Conscious Dancer Magazine*

"Makes a special contribution to the world of mindfulness by inviting all of us to get off the cushion and explore moving our miraculous bodies.… I encourage anyone interested in mindfulness to let go of old inhibitions and follow Jamie's wonderful guidance to experience the full body/mind joy of mindful dancing."

—Terry Fralich, co-founder, Mindfulness Retreat Center of Maine;
author, *The Five Core Skills of Mindfulness:
A Direct Path to More Confidence, Joy and Love*

"Offers a pathway to spirit through the body. Each chapter offers a doorway to dancing mindfulness as a personal practice and as an opportunity to facilitate others.… A must-read for anyone interested in developing a mindfulness practice through dance."

—Theresa Benson, PhD, licensed clinical psychologist;
expressive arts facilitator, University of Illinois

"Meditation is more than sitting on your butt. Mindfulness is more than obsessively chewing a raisin. Both are about being so physically present to the environment that you can no longer maintain the delusion that you are other than the environment. [This book and practice] will take you to that place of acute presentness, and awaken you to the dance of life within and without."

—Rabbi Rami Shapiro, author, *Perennial Wisdom for the Spiritually Independent: Sacred Teachings—Annotated & Explained*

"Will help you dance your story in your space with mindfulness—a journey home to the present moment and ultimately to your authentic self … greatly aided by the richness of intentional movement."

—Durga Leela, RYT-500, founder, *Yoga of Recovery*

"Helps us step away from the idea that in order to practice living mindfully or to 'figure things out' we should sit cross-legged, empty our minds and wait for answers. Our true ability to be mindful can come through dance and movement whenever we let it ... the possibilities are endless and so is your capacity for love, strength and acceptance. To quote Jamie, 'get up and dance!'"

—Rev. Donald McCasland, LMSW-CCTP, clinical trauma professional; blogger, "The Functional Veteran"

"An exciting new way to becoming fully present [and] a powerful introduction to a sense of total wellness.... I recommend this book most highly. This is mindfulness in spades—five stars."

—Rev. Paschal Baute, EdD, author, *Resilience of a Dream Catcher, Secrets of Intimacy* and *Lottie Mae, The Turkey Who Could Not Stop Dreaming*

"The modern gateway to the mind/body consciousness.... Reminds us to get up and feel our lives as they were meant to be *alive* in mind, body and spirit. Of course, the real gem ... is that it's even deeper than being *alive*—it's being down right joyful about it."

—Leisa T. Mills, Buddhist teacher and mind/body activist

"Most interesting ... for those looking for a more physical and creative way to practice mindfulness.... Includes discussion of the historical significance of dance as a healing arts form that involves attention to the physical and emotional self and, when practiced in a group, to growth in community and community building. The book also provides guidance in workshop development and leadership in this method, and has a DVD to illustrate the method."

—Christine A. Courtois, PhD, ABPP, psychologist, Washington, DC; author, *It's Not You, It's What Happened to You; Healing the Incest Wound* and *Treating Complex Trauma: A Sequenced, Relationship-based Approach* (with Julian Ford, PhD)

Dancing
mindfulness

A Creative
Path to Healing &
Transformation

JAMIE MARICH, PhD, LPCC-S

FOREWORD BY CHRISTINE VALTERS PAINTNER, PhD, OBL. OSB, REACE

Walking Together, Finding the Way®
SKYLIGHT PATHS®
PUBLISHING
Nashville, Tennessee

Dancing Mindfulness:
A Creative Path to Healing and Transformation

For information regarding permission to reprint material from this book, please write or fax your request to SkyLight Paths Publishing, Permissions Department, at the address / fax number listed below, or e-mail your request to permissions@skylightpaths.com.

Grateful acknowledgment is given for permission to use material from *The Essential Rumi, New Expanded Edition* by Jalal al-Din Rumi, translation by Coleman Barks, published by HarperOne, © 2004. Used by permission of Coleman Barks.

Library of Congress Cataloging-in-Publication Data
Marich, Jamie.
    Dancing mindfulness : a creative path to healing and transformation / Jamie Marich, PhD, LPCC-S ; foreword by Christine Valters Paintner, PhD, Obl. OSB, REACE. — 2015 quality paperback edition.
        pages cm
    Includes bibliographical references and index.
    ISBN 978-1-59473-601-8 (pbk.) — ISBN 978-1-59473-607-0 (ebook) — ISBN 978-1-68336-021-6 (hc) 1. Dance therapy. I. Title.
    RC489.D3M37 2015
    616.89'1655—dc23

                                2015027768

Manufactured in the United States of America
Cover Design: Jenny Buono
Interior Design: Tim Holtz
Cover Art: © Patrizia Tilly/Shutterstock

SkyLight Paths Publishing is creating a place where people of different spiritual traditions come together for challenge and inspiration, a place where we can help each other understand the mystery that lies at the heart of our existence.

SkyLight Paths sees both believers and seekers as a community that increasingly transcends traditional boundaries of religion and denomination—people wanting to learn from each other, *walking together, finding the way.*

Walking Together, Finding the Way®
Published by SkyLight Paths Publishing
An imprint of Turner Publishing Company
4507 Charlotte Avenue, Suite 100
Nashville, TN 37209
Tel: (615) 255-2665
www.skylightpaths.com

I dedicate this book to the first formally trained class of *Dancing Mindfulness* facilitators—thank you for asking me to put this all down on paper and train you eleven amazing ladies! It's because of you that the practice is growing into what it is. Dance on!

In memory of Linda Johnson (d. 2014), a proud, glowing member of the first *Dancing Mindfulness* training class. Linda embodied the concept of dancing her joy, and she touched all of us who had the privilege of training with her during that first class. I look forward to the glorious day when we can dance again together on the other side!

Contents

Foreword

Christine Valters Paintner

I first got to know Jamie and her work when I found her *Dancing Mindfulness* website online. For many years I have loved the power of dance to bring me back to the present moment and into the wisdom of my body. I have studied several practices of what is known as conscious dance, dance that doesn't have "steps" but is more an invitation into the organic and spontaneous movement of the body. These practices have included 5Rhythms, founded by Gabrielle Roth; SoulMotion, founded by Vinn Marti; BodySoul Rhythms, founded by Marion Woodman and Ann Skinner; and InterPlay, founded by Cynthia Winton Henry and Phil Porter.

These systems are all powerful and wonderfully complex. I was drawn to Jamie's work for its simplicity and fundamental connection between movement practice and mindfulness meditation. When she offered her *Dancing Mindfulness* training in an online format, I took the opportunity to learn more from her, especially from her gifts as a trauma specialist. Jamie herself is full of the intelligence and compassion her work expresses. I deeply appreciated our conversations about the healing power of dance and ways to keep participants as safe and grounded as possible.

It was an even greater gift when Jamie attended a movement retreat I led called "Coming Home to Your Body," and we got to dance together in physical reality, as opposed to just virtual reality.

ix

I delighted in her obvious commitment to her own practice and process, never shying away from the depth work of her own journey. This to me is a key indicator of the integrity and strength of a teacher: how much she or he is committed to doing their own inner work. Jamie offered much wisdom to our community; this arose from her own self-reflection and willingness to share her tenderness and moments of new awareness.

Jamie's gift to the world in this *Dancing Mindfulness* work is an invitation and a portal into the practice of dance and movement as meditation. All bodies are welcome and all abilities. Anyone can dance, although many of us hold back because we don't look like dancers or because we have physical limitations. But I am willing to bet that most of you holding this book have touched a moment of transcendence or freedom in an experience of dance that leads you to explore deeper. You have a worthy guide in your hands.

Jamie elegantly weaves mindfulness principles into her practice so that anyone with a body might discover the grace and possibilities of this practice. The Buddhist writer Reginald Ray has a book titled *Touching Enlightenment: Finding Realization in the Body*, in which he describes the body as "the last unexplored wilderness." I personally find this image very compelling, and *Dancing Mindfulness* offers a map into this place of wilderness and wisdom. Never rigid, always fluid, Jamie invites you to find your own dance, your own practice.

INTRODUCTION

The Art of Dancing Mindfully

Dance, when you're broken open. Dance, if you've torn the bandage off. Dance in the middle of the fighting. Dance in your blood. Dance when you're perfectly free.

—*Rumi*

What images do you associate with the word *mindfulness*?

Do you see a fit yogi meditating on a beach in a perfect lotus position, entranced by the surrounding calm? Or do you picture a saintly Buddhist monk, eyes closed, clutching his prayer beads? Maybe you see a large group of people gathered at a festival, chanting *Om* in unison. You might even envision someone taking deliberate steps through a garden labyrinth, savoring each pace of a walking meditation. As mainstream as the practice of mindfulness has become in the last twenty years, our images of how to be mindful are still pretty cliché. If you don't believe me, go to your favorite Internet search engine and type in the word *mindfulness*.

Here's a new image to try out: a dance floor full of people. Picture a community of people of all shapes, sizes, and physical abilities, each of them connecting their individual body, mind, and spirit through the simplest of rhythmic movements. A gathering of beings, getting down and grooving to every musical genre imaginable in one moment, and then shifting to the stillness of standing or sitting with an experience in the next. A collection of souls, each with their own unique story to tell, having fun and being themselves in the moment, tapping into the fullness of their human potential. This is dancing mindfulness.

What Is Mindfulness? What Is Dance?

Every human activity can be engaged mindfully—eating, stretching, breathing, walking, singing, praying, speaking, kissing, hugging, love-making, star gazing, and buying your groceries. So why not dancing?

There are a variety of ways to experience mindful awareness and to cultivate its practice. *Mindfulness* derives from the Sanskrit word *smriti*, meaning "awareness." In a more nuanced translation, *smriti* means "to come back to awareness." Jon Kabat-Zinn, a visionary who brings ancient mindfulness concepts to Western healthcare, simply defines mindfulness as "paying attention in a particular way: on purpose, in the presence of the moment, and non-judgmentally."[1] A task force of scholars, assembled to draft a concise explanation of mindfulness, offered the following definition: the self-regulation of attention to the conscious awareness of one's immediate experiences while adopting an attitude of curiosity, openness, and acceptance.[2] A yoga teacher I know puts the concept into even simpler terms during her class. The teacher invites us, in each pose, to "be a witness, not a judge."

Like mindfulness, dance has been revered as an intrinsically heal-ing art form by various cultures across the continents and across millennia of human existence. Dance promotes the building of com-munity, is phenomenal physical exercise, and serves as a powerful communication medium. Yes, before there were Facebook groups, people used communal dancing as a way to gather and to learn about each other. This sacred art is still alive and well in many cultures and communities. Dancing is a coping skill for stress relief. Dance is a practice that native and indigenous cultures use, in lieu of talking, for total healing following a traumatic experience. Asian, Middle Eastern, and African cultures call upon movement, including certain types of dance, as a healing art form. Even traditional folklore in many European cultures incorporates these beneficial qualities. I would know, since such folklore provided my introduction to dancing!

Yet, in modern Western cultures, we tend to be inhibited when it comes to dancing. We fear that if we don't dance well we really shouldn't be dancing at all. We are victims of the "looks are everything" mentality. We do a whole lot of judging—of others and especially of ourselves—and not a lot of witnessing. What if we combined the beauty of mindful practice with nonjudgmental movement? Imagine the healing potential we could realize—for ourselves as well as in our roles as helping professionals working in community or clinical settings. Tapping into our potential for movement, creating beauty, and achieving mindful awareness defines a dancing mindfulness practice. Through such a practice we learn to respond to the needs of our body, mind, and spirit. Responding to these needs, instead of reacting compulsively or withdrawing into isolation, leads to enhanced wellness, vitality, and clarity.

Try This: Practicing Seated Awareness

- Shift around in your chair a little bit, or in a seated position on the ground, until you find a position that, for you, symbolizes paying attention.

- Be careful not to slouch, but also be aware not to sit up so straight that it hurts you to be in this sitting posture.

- Spend some time paying attention to your body and make a mental note of what this posture of awareness feels like to you.

- If your mind starts to wander or you feel that you've stopped paying attention, that's okay; it doesn't mean you are doing this incorrectly. When you catch yourself, just use this as a chance to bring your attention back to that body posture of awareness. Mindfulness is about the coming back, the coming home to awareness.

- Begin this practice for any time interval (even a few seconds is okay). Try easing into practicing this seated awareness for at least three to five minutes. As your practice grows, notice if you are able to spend longer periods in seated awareness.

Modifications

- If you try doing this for three minutes and simply can't do it, consider adding in another sensory element and practice paying attention to that element (a scent, like an oil, a spice, or a candle; a simple sound, like something from a nature sounds CD; or a tactile sensation, like holding a rock, a marble, or a stuffed animal).

- If sitting doesn't work, this same exercise can also be done standing up or lying down. Remember to keep the emphasis on that word *awareness*. You can lie down with awareness.

My Journey with Dance, Recovery, and Mindfulness

My parents met in Slavic folk dancing troupes, decades before Internet dating and computer-based social networking even existed. Both sets of my great-grandparents emigrated from Croatia. They carried on the cultural elements of their homeland here in the United States by enrolling their children in Croatian folk dancing and musical groups called Tamburitzans. My mother belonged to one in Youngstown, Ohio, and my father was a member of a Cleveland troupe (some sixty miles away). The two of them met at a national festival that brought young people together from all over the United States and Canada. So, quite literally, I am here because of folk music and dancing!

Thus it's appropriate that my first orientation to dancing was at age four, when I joined the very same folk group to which my mother belonged. Fun, bouncy *kolos* (circle dances) were a staple of my childhood, and my first exposure to anything theatrical or psycho-dramatic occurred when I took part in these finely choreographed traditional dances. My first "wedding" was during such a dance, as I had the privilege of playing the bride in the Wedding Dances from Posavina (a region of Croatia) at age twelve. Although it was awkward to "marry" Georgie, a kid I grew up with and generally despised, I look back on the experience now as a special memory of my child-hood. Not only were we having fun, but we were also carrying on the legacy of our people here in the United States.

Later in my childhood I started figure skating, and I took ballet and jazz classes to help me develop lyrical expression. Even though I trained for thousands of hours in all these formats, I never once called myself a *dancer*. At best, I was a skater who danced, but that label of *dancer* was somehow reserved only for people who were good enough to dance professionally.

As an adult, I stopped taking formal dance classes, yet I was always the first one to get up at weddings and move when the band started. As a successful professional in my late twenties, after several years in recov-ery from trauma-based depression and addiction, I sought to explore my unfulfilled desire to move. I enrolled in a local ballroom dancing program, but ultimately found it too expensive and too limiting, since I did not have a regular partner who wanted to dance with me.

Then I discovered yoga. Learning the practice helped me better listen to my body, and it transformed my approach to personal recov-ery. I connected with a local studio in Warren, Ohio, near my home. Through the two primary teachers at this amazing place, including my first yoga mentor, Maureen, I experienced the joy of a "come as you are" community where age, weight, body type, or level of yoga experience does not matter. As Maureen always teaches, carrying on the tradition of her own training, "If you can breathe, you can do yoga." I remain forever grateful to her for the welcoming, accepting, noncompetitive atmosphere she creates at her studio.

But as much as I embraced yoga, I still found that there was some-thing missing. It was then that I discovered conscious dance. At nine years sober, I signed up for a weekend yoga retreat led by a writer I admired. I found myself taking one of the noon classes in "Conscious Dance," a genre generally defined as movement with an intention toward higher awareness.[3] I was hooked! Each day there were many brands of conscious dance led by different facilitators knowledgeable in yogic language. They were usually fantastic dancers themselves, and able to foster empowerment in the participants. People of all skill levels can dance consciously and, unlike other forms out there, there is absolutely no pressure to know certain steps. You just listen to the facilitator and go with it. As I moved with ease across the floor in a way I hadn't since I was a child, I was finally able to own the phrase "I *am* a dancer!"

Having people tell me that they were inspired by the way I danced, even with my larger body stature, prompted me to lead these types of conscious dance classes myself. It came to me as an instant inner knowing: if someone who isn't a perfect body type can lead a dance class, perhaps even more people who are hung up on their inhibitions and vicious self-judgments would get up and dance.

Because, to me, dance is the quintessential way to experience mindful awareness and practice meditation, I developed the practice of dancing mindfulness. Dancing mindfulness differs from many other conscious dance forms in that I do not prescribe a specific flow that you have to follow of various rhythms or dance choices. How you structure your practice is completely up to you, as long as you warm up at the beginning; dance to a deeper, exploratory place in the middle (how deep you go is completely up to you); and ultimately cool down physically as well as settle emotionally. Dancing mindfulness offers seven core elements with which you can practice:

- **Breath.** The basic essence of animal life. Being attuned to the power of breath is a vital doorway to mindful awareness. Checking in with your breath is critical in the dancing mindfulness practice, and mindful attunement to the breath gives you excellent information about your relationship to the practice and its depth at any given moment.

- **Sound.** The vibration of life most often associated with the sense of hearing. But sound can also be channeled in a tactile manner. Sound can refer to the music that guides your practice, and it can also refer to the tones generated by breath, heartbeat, and motions like stomping your feet on the floor, clapping your hands, or chanting.

- **Body.** The container of our physical experience. Honoring the body and the information it gives you about emotional content is vital to practicing mindful awareness, especially when engaging in a process as physically engaging as dance.

- **Mind.** The information processing system in human beings, the outlet through which we take in and send out information; the mechanism of humanity that makes mindful awareness possible. When stress or negativity grips you, the mind is generally holding on to undigested information. Unwarranted negative beliefs and old patterns, ingrained in the mind, fuel the fire of stressors. However, just as the mind can hold on to negativity, so too can our attitudes be transformed to focus more on the positive.

- **Spirit.** The realm of experience that cannot be explained by the scientific laws of nature; that which is greater than you or I. Some people access the spiritual world through religion. Others tap into the cosmic flow of the universe; still others forge a relationship with their chosen Higher Power(s).

- **Story.** The narrative of experience, which can be manifested and expressed in a variety of ways. Stories can be told in the first, second, or third person. Stories can be the lived experience of the mindful dancer, or a character who emerges during a given dance. In the dancing mindfulness practice, genuineness must guide the telling of your story, and that story must be told in an atmosphere of nonjudgment.

- **Fusion.** The coming together of all of these elements—the vital integration that allows us to experience a greater sense of renewal, rest, and wholeness. There are several places in the dancing mindfulness practice where this integration can occur. However, during a period of reflection and rest at the end of the practice, your experience crystallizes into transformative insight.

There are various ways to incorporate each element into a dance flow. In personal practice it may happen organically. In a class setting it may be guided by a facilitator.

At present, I facilitate hour- to hour-and-a-half-long classes within community settings, like yoga studios or health and wellness fairs, and I have also had the pleasure of facilitating classes on retreats and with my professional colleagues at both local and national conferences. In the first three years of *Dancing Mindfulness*'s* existence as a formal practice, a diverse group of one hundred women came forward to receive training as facilitators.

Vanessa Boglio, a Puerto Rican psychologist, had experience with dance, but not dance as meditation, before arriving at her own facilitator training. She summarizes her reaction:

> For me dancing mindfulness is being free in the moment, enjoying good music, and most important, liberating oneself from inhibitions, stress, and negativity. We all have insecurities, pain, hurt, traumas, but by dancing mindfully, with acceptance and no judgment of our decisions, our behaviors, our mistakes, we find tranquility, peace, harmony. Dancing mindfulness is a great practice to better our physical and emotional state.

---

*Author's Note: When you see "dancing mindfulness" written as such throughout the book (not capitalized, no italics), I am referencing the practice of dance as a way to access and cultivate mindful awareness. When you see *Dancing Mindfulness* written with initial capital letters and italics, I am referencing the systematized practice that you may choose to facilitate with groups of people.

Try This: How Do You Define *Dance*?

When I conduct trainings, I generally ask people to consider their starting point—their existing definition of some concept—before moving forward with a training or, in this case, the book. So I ask you to do the same: At your gut level, how would you define dance?

Here is what a couple of my friends and colleagues shared:

Uninhibited movement of self.

Bruno Mars at the Super Bowl.

Shakin' it until you're happy.

Allowing the music to "move" me.

Your body listening to the beat of your heart.

An expression of your soul.

Setting one's spirit free!

Flow of movements and stillness of the body to inner and/or outer sounds of rhythm.

I can't define it with words, only with movement.

Dancing Mindfulness versus Dance Therapy

I recently spoke with a friend who directs a state-of-the-art trauma treatment program in Tennessee. Being so close to the vibrancy of Nashville and its music scene, he is in a position to implement some creative collaboration between Nashville songwriters and the people his program serves. He explained to me, "What we do isn't music therapy in a technical sense. I've read the books on music therapy and find what it teaches to be far too limited and structured." As soon as he shared this with me, I felt as if someone finally grasped what I was saying about the differences between dancing mindfulness and dance therapy. My essential position is that dancing mindfulness is not dance therapy, a formal field of study developed by Marian Chace in the 1950s. Although many practitioners of dancing mindfulness find it to be therapeutic or healing, dancing mindfulness is fundamentally a meditation practice that uses dance as the primary means of achieving mindful awareness. Dancing mindfulness may be practiced on your own, shared in the community, or brought into clinical or healthcare settings if such settings are open to meditation.

According to Jon Kabat-Zinn, meditation is any activity that helps us systematically regulate our attention and energy. Meditation influences and sometimes transforms the quality of our experience to help us realize the full range of our humanity and of our relationship to others in the world.[4] Rezvan Ameli, another leader in secular mindfulness, describes the two major components of mindfulness as (1) focused attention and (2) a quality of openness and positivity in the heart.[5] There are many ways to meditate, with different approaches having nuanced effects for those who practice it.[6] Buddhist teacher Martine Batchelor conducted interviews with Asian women—both nuns and laywomen. She concluded that the specific techniques of meditation used do not seem to matter as much as a person's sincerity in practicing the dharma, or "the body of principles and practices that sustain human beings in their quest for happiness and spiritual freedom."[7] As a woman who benefits from mindful practices yet has no desire to become a Buddhist or adopt a strict Buddhist approach to mindfulness, I feel that Batchelor's conclusion makes a great deal of sense. I also draw inspiration and hope from a well-known teaching of His Holiness the Dalai Lama. He says, "Don't become a Buddhist. The world doesn't need more Buddhists. Do practice compassion. The world needs more compassion."[8]

Kabat-Zinn, whose work introduced me to the basics of mindfulness and how to apply it outside of purely Buddhist contexts, contends that there are seven primary attitudes that we can acquire and further cultivate through a regular practice of mindfulness.[9] These attitudes are:

- nonjudgment

- patience

- beginner's mind

- nonstriving

- trust

- acceptance

- letting go

Let's consider what each of these attitudes means as they relate to movement. As you read the explanations, ask yourself how fully embracing each attitude might have a positive impact on your life. Think about how moving in the moment may help you to more fully embrace each attitude.

Nonjudgment

Being nonjudgmental of your internal processes is at the heart of mindfulness practice. Nonjudging refers to thinking, feeling, or responding without the influence of an internal sensor or critic. Nonjudging is an attitude of "just noticing" thoughts, emotions, or whatever may surface as relevant. Nonjudgment, however, does not endorse behaviors that put yourself or others in harm's way. For instance, consider a recovering addict who is experiencing an intense craving to use a substance following a stressful day. Nonjudgment does not advocate that he should go out and use, which would certainly be harmful. Rather, nonjudgment encourages him to just notice the craving, pay attention to it, and be with it in a spirit of nonjudgment. By doing that, we are more likely to make the healthier choice on how to handle something like a craving instead of beating ourselves up for having the craving. This scenario plays out time and time again with recovering people: we beat ourselves up for having an unhealthy thought or craving, this leads to shame, and shameful feelings tend to be the biggest trigger for unhealthy behaviors.

Patience

Mindfulness, especially if practiced regularly, helps us become more patient with ourselves. *Patience*, which derives from the Latin root meaning to "undergo," "suffer," or "bear," is the art of deferring gratification. Patience teaches us how to wait with grace. By cultivating this attitude, not only do we learn to defer instant gratification but we can also learn to be gentler with ourselves when old, shame-based responses rear their heads and attempt to sabotage our wellness. Mindfulness practice is a way that we can work with and ultimately transform the old beliefs and emotional responses that no longer serve us. In his work *Resilience of a Dream Catcher: A Spiritual Memoir*, my workshop collaborator and friend, clinical psychologist Dr. Paschal Baute, explains the link between mindfulness and the process of making us more resilient:

> Mindfulness is openness to embrace whatever life presents, with awareness of the possibilities of the moment. It is an awakening to the full awareness. *Resilience* is the act of transcending and transforming that moment, threat, challenge or loss. Much overlap exists. *Being mindful is already an act of transcending one's circumstances.*[10]

Beginner's Mind

Beginner's mind is the mindfulness attitude at play when it comes to retraining the brain. *Beginner* comes from the same Middle English root as "to open." Thus, beginner's mind is approaching each new task with an open mind. Think of the sense of wonder that a child may experience when trying something new. With this attitude, we remove an expert's mind-set and refrain from living on metaphorical autopilot. Practices like walking meditation are wonderful strategies to work with beginner's mind, since we are challenged to take an activity that we tend to do without thinking, like walking, and break it down to appreciate each individual part, as if we were walking for the first time. At a yoga retreat I attended, a teacher suggested the following: the slower you take a movement, the more you notice about that movement. His teaching resonated immediately and helped me to practice beginner's mind with a flowing pose that I'd done a thousand times before. His suggestion to slow it down made it new again.

Nonstriving

Practicing any activity with a beginner's mind is also a wonderful way to practice nonstriving: thinking, feeling, or acting with focus on the process, not just the outcome. The name of this skill confuses many people because in Western culture we tend to associate nonstriving with giving up. Nonstriving does not imply laziness or sloth. Nonstriving is an attitude that encourages you, even in your work, to refrain from trying so hard. In nonstriving, we let whatever happens, happen. As the well-worn cliché goes, life is about the journey, not the destination. Yet this saying encapsulates the spirit of nonstriving. My first recovery sponsor, Janet, pointed out my tendency to fixate on the end result. This behavior stemmed from two decades of pushing myself within a Western culture defined by achievement and high performance. She asked me this question early on in our work together: "What would happen if you just enjoyed the process?" My initial reaction was to wince, as if I would somehow betray my work ethic by doing that. What I eventually learned is that the reward is in the process, and learning to enjoy it instead of obsessing over the outcome yields more rewards, especially in the existential sense, than I ever thought possible. For me, a sense of peace with my life is proving to be the ultimate reward, a major fruit of just being with and trusting the process.

Trust, Acceptance, and Letting Go

The final three attitudes also help us enjoy the journey without letting the stress of reaching the destination trouble us. First, there is the attitude of trust, or believing in some unseen entity, another person or group, or the internal self. We can also practice trust in the journey.

Then there is acceptance, or coming to terms with reality, no matter how harsh or unpleasant it may be. Practicing acceptance can be a pathway to peace. Acceptance does not imply that you have to "like" the reality that you discontinue fighting. Acceptance is internalizing the attitude of *It is what it is*.

Finally, there is the attitude of letting go, or releasing your "grip" on a situation, emotion, person, thing, or outcome. Letting go generally makes us feel liberated—or at least as if freedom is close at hand. This response can clear the path for our own wellness and growth.

According to Kabat-Zinn, these seven primary attitudes are the foundational fruits of mindfulness practice. By internalizing them, a variety of other attitudes can flow into our lives, such as friendliness, gratitude, gentleness, curiosity, nonattachment, nonreactivity, happiness, and creativity. Others may include attunement, persistence, confidence, and willingness. Attunement, or being in harmony with another human being or entity, is an especially vital skill for helping professionals or those facilitating community *Dancing Mindfulness* practices. Attunement allows us to more effectively read a person's nonverbal signals and sense any subtle shifts in energy or relationship dynamics. For instance, listening to that inner prompting in your gut that one of the dancers in your community class just isn't feeling safe or comfortable may lead you to check in, either verbally or nonverbally, with that practitioner. You may be able to tell at the body level that something much deeper is bothering a client or someone you see for spiritual direction, even though they say everything is okay. Examples of enhanced attunement's positive impact on our work with others are endless.

Try This: The Attitudes of Mindfulness—Personal Reflection & Practice

- You may already feel comfortable with at least one of the attitudes of mindful practice. If so, take that attitude and spend a moment in seated awareness just noticing what that attitude means to you, not judging your process.

- Allow yourself to move with that attitude in a way that feels right and organic for you, just noticing what happens.

- To guide your moving meditation, you may ask yourself, "What does my dance of trust look like or feel like?" If you feel that cuing up some music that represents your chosen attitude would help inspire you, go ahead and do that.

- After you have spent some time moving with an attitude that is familiar to you, I challenge you to repeat this process with an attitude that is a struggle for you at this moment in your life. Notice whatever it is that surfaces, remembering that the goal is not to create a perfect dance or even a perfect experience. Just be with the process.

While mindfulness practice may seem simple on the surface, practicing it can be quite challenging. Western society is the very definition of *mindlessness*, and this modern-day reality compounds the challenge of living mindfully. We are fast-paced and results-oriented. We are focused on the "doing" rather than the "being." For those of us raised in Western culture, adopting a mindful lifestyle through mindfulness practice represents a major paradigm shift. Dancing mindfulness offers us a creative practice for moving through such a shift and hopefully discovering transformation in the process.

How to Use This Book

If you've picked up this book, it is likely that the concept of dancing mindfulness piqued your interest. Perhaps you are devoted to mindful practice and expanding its possibilities. I hope that if you are in this group, you will absorb what you read and perhaps be inspired to turn on your home stereo or iPod and move around a little bit. Experiment. Explore. Be in the moment with your movement! Play around with making dancing mindfulness part of your personal meditation or wellness practice. Dance is a legitimate form of meditation, and I hope to provide you with several ideas for how to integrate dance and movement into meditation practice.

If you come from a very traditional mindfulness background, steeped in traditional Buddhist thought, you may struggle with some elements of this book—maybe all of it. Echoing the words of many modern-day mindfulness luminaries, there is nothing inherently Buddhist about the practice of mindfulness. For instance, I identify as a Christian who is inspired by teachings from many world religions, including Buddhism. Dancing mindfulness, as I practice it, is a modern twist on the ancient practice that works for me, a non-Buddhist raised in Western culture. It is a testament to the idea that you don't have to become Buddhist or abandon your own faith traditions to practice mindfulness.

Dancing Mindfulness is a reinvention and reintegration of time-honored traditions and learning from the psychotherapeutic professions on how to best heal trauma and manage stress. It offers a path for cultivating and practicing mindful awareness; it is not a brand of conscious dance or a trademark. Many of us practice *Dancing Mindfulness* in classes or group settings, similar to how a *sangha* gathers for seated meditation practice. Others primarily practice dancing mindfulness as a personal venture to achieve wellness. Growing numbers of us practice dancing mindfulness in both group settings and as personal practice, discovering that dancing mindfulness can become a way of life. I recently visited with *Dancing Mindfulness* facilitator Lexie Rae, a woman based in Columbus, Ohio, who is passionate about dance and embracing her inner child. Simply put, dancing with Lexie is a splendid experience. She often comes to *Dancing Mindfulness* classes wearing fun costume elements, like tutus, superhero capes, or hilarious T-shirts sporting phrases like *Twerk It Out*. Lexie acknowledges that she moves with elements of dancing mindfulness in daily life and they define her life and her wellness. She doesn't need to attend or teach classes to embrace dancing mindfulness elements and attitudes as a lifestyle, as a creative path to present-centered living.

You practice dancing mindfulness whenever you adhere to mindfulness attitudes or at least set them as an intention in your movement. You are practicing dancing mindfulness whenever your movement can inspire others to get up and move, allowing them to create their own special moments. Considering this definition, you can even practice dancing mindfulness on Facebook by inspiring others through your embrace of the practice as a way of life. One day I received a lovely note from a professional colleague of mine, Dr. Andrew Dobo. Although he follows me on Facebook, I had no idea that he was being stirred into movement by seeing the posts that I share with others in the *Dancing Mindfulness* community. He shared that he was dancing around his kitchen to one of his favorite groups, Chicago 36. Andrew mused: "I'm an introvert who doesn't dance, but I'm trying to follow your lead. Dancing is always a good idea." Andrew's experience reaffirms the wisdom of a centuries-old Swahili proverb: "He who dances at home will be rewarded."

Promoting experimentation with personal practice in dancing mindfulness is the main focus of this book. Although you are welcome to just read the text, you will be in a better position to internalize it if you engage in some of this experimentation. Throughout this book, "Try This" exercises provide prompts and suggestions for developing your own dancing mindfulness practice in your home, your office, or wherever you have the space to practice.

Chapters 1 through 7 dive in to the seven core elements of the *Dancing Mindfulness* practice as I am defining it. These chapters will be the most relevant if you are primarily reading this book for personal growth and self-practice of dancing mindfulness. In these chapters, I reflect on each element—breath, sound, body, mind, spirit, story, and fusion. Explaining how each element can play out in a dancing mindfulness experience, I call upon stories from my own development as both a performing artist and a psychotherapist. I reference the teachings of those who most influenced me in my journey to mindfully dance these elements, and I discuss how the people I facilitate teach me about each element and the practice as a whole. In my academic

life, I was a qualitative researcher, meaning that I am in love with stories, themes, and concepts, and these three passions are highlighted in
this work. In each chapter, the "Try This" prompts encourage experimentation for personal practice and offer user-friendly instructions
that would-be facilitators can use in their classes as starting points, in
addition to musical suggestions for each element.

Perhaps you are feeling the desire to lead others in a *Dancing Mindfulness* practice. Chapter 8 sets some of the parameters of what con-
stitute the safest, most fulfilling *Dancing Mindfulness* experiences for
people. I present some of the ways in which communities are gathering to practice *Dancing Mindfulness*, which may inspire ideas for
your own wellness group or spiritual community. This chapter also
includes tips on developing skills as a facilitator.

You may ask, "But can I facilitate *Dancing Mindfulness* just by reading this book?" There's no hard-and-fast answer to this question
because all of you are so different. If you are a yoga teacher, a dance
instructor, a ministry leader, or a helping professional who has experience guiding people, the chances are highly likely that you will easily assume the leadership role in *Dancing Mindfulness*. Listen to your
inner voice. If you have no prior leadership experience, particularly
with body-mind-spirit practices, you may find additional training
helpful. I developed a weekend-long facilitator training format for
people interested in gaining direct instructional experience, and I
offer distance-based mentorships at the request of international students. Trust your judgment and/or consult with someone you trust on
what you most need as a would-be facilitator of *Dancing Mindfulness*.

A key piece of information I wish to impart right here as we open
the book is that there is no *right* way to practice dancing mindfulness.
Although I do not describe *Dancing Mindfulness* as a specifically clinical practice or approach to psychotherapy, it certainly can be taken
into clinical settings as an activity, or well-trained professionals may
apply it clinically alongside other therapeutic approaches. I see this
clinical application as ripe for exploration, since *Dancing Mindfulness*
foundations are rooted in well-established clinical knowledge about

mindfulness, trauma recovery, and human behavior. If you are compelled to carry *Dancing Mindfulness* into clinical settings, get in touch with our community about your progress at www.dancingmindfulness.com. We'd love to hear what you're doing!

The key to a successful group *Dancing Mindfulness* practice is the fusion between four components—the authentic self of the facilitator, the needs of the group requiring facilitation, the setting and purpose of the class, and the ability of the facilitator to gauge the needs of the group. Thus, how I teach a class will be completely different from how you teach a class, and I *love* that. To me, that's what makes *Dancing Mindfulness* special. I fully recognize that the students I end up training in *Dancing Mindfulness* may lead more dynamic, powerful classes than I ever could. In fact, I hope you all will! Thus, in chapter 8 I reflect on the fusion of these four components referenced here and how they all go into making a class your own. At the end of the book, I offer resources that you may find helpful in your journey to share the practice. These resources include ways to connect with *Dancing Mindfulness* and related communities online.

My sincerest hope is that, in one way or another, you will get up and dance! Enjoy each movement you are able to produce in each splendid moment. Above all else, embrace the art of dance as a legitimate form of meditation, a creative path for living your life as a witness, not a judge.

Try This: Personal Reflection & Practice

Whether the prospect of dancing mindfully scares you or excites you, I invite you to engage in this simple experiment:

- Take one of your hands and raise it above your head. If raising it all the way above your head is not physically possible, go as far as you can. This is not a contest.

- Inhale as you lift your hand above your head or away from your body.

- On your next exhale, slowly, deliberately, and mindfully allow your hand to float back down to your side. Repeat as many times as you wish.

- In this simple experiment, see if you can practice being a witness and not a judge.

Other Voices

Fralich, Terry. *The Five Core Skills of Mindfulness: A Direct Path to More Confidence, Joy, and Love*. Eau Claire, WI: PESI Publishing and Media, 2013.

Hanh, Thich Nhat, and Arnold Kotler. *Peace Is Every Step: The Path of Mindfulness in Everyday Life*. New York: Bantam, 1992.

Kabat-Zinn, Jon. *Mindfulness for Beginners: Reclaiming the Present Moment—and Your Life*. Boulder, CO: Sounds True Books, 2011.

Some Basics Before You Get Started

As you begin exploring dancing mindfulness as a practice, take the following suggestions into consideration for your own health and safety:

- **Footwear and Apparel.** On a hardwood floor, I usually advise participants to dance barefoot. You may feel more comfortable initially in your socks. However, proceed with caution if you want to keep your socks on when you come into standing movement. Socks can be slippery on smooth surfaces. Of course, dance shoes of any kind—basic ballet slippers, jazz shoes—generally work on hardwood surfaces. On carpet or other surfaces, the footwear issue is rarely a major consideration. You want to be comfortable, yet mindful of your safety in movement. The same goes for apparel. You can wear anything you like when practicing dancing mindfulness. If you are going to engage in longer practices, the key is to dress in a way that allows for physical comfort in movement. To keep from tripping, don't wear pants that are too long.

- **Being Mindful of Mindfulness.** Mindfulness is simply about noticing experience without judgment and honoring what comes up. So, knowing this, there isn't a right or wrong way to do dancing mindfulness, as long as you are present with your experience. Remember that if your attention wanders outside the room and away from your dance, that doesn't mean you are doing this wrong. The practice is in noticing when your attention drifts and then drawing it back to the present moment.

- **Honoring Your Limits.** Listen to your body throughout the practice and avoid pushing yourself further than your body can safely go. While the practice may inspire you to push harder, especially if you are in a group and see others dancing, listening to when your body says "too much" is vital in avoiding injury.

- **Opting Out Is Always an Option.** If you need to leave your dance space to get a drink of water, or to take a moment to rest or reflect, do so. Honoring a need for rest and stillness is a vital part of dancing mindfully.

- **Ensuring Emotional Safety.** Sometimes dance can be an emotional experience. Having someone you can connect with if distress arises—by phone, email, an online forum, or Skype—may be comforting as you move more deeply into the practice.

Chapter 1

Breath

Life Dancing Through Us

The mind is king of the senses, and the breath is the king of
the mind.

—*Swami Svātmārāma*, Hatha Yoga Pradipika

Absent any major health issues, the typical adult takes anywhere
from fifteen to twenty breaths each minute—on the lower end that
makes twenty thousand breaths a day.[1] Each year, that tally is anywhere from 7 million to 8 million complete cycles of inhale-exhale
per person. Consider how many breaths you've already taken in your
lifetime. We pass through our days with our lungs pumping on autopilot, sustaining life. But how often do we stop to take a mindful
pause and harness our breath's full potential? Do we ever pause to
contemplate the wonder of what's happening in our bodies as we
inhale and exhale? What if we could learn to cherish our breath as life
itself dancing through our being?

I've gained much experience teaching people how to breathe deeply
and fully in my professional vocation as a counselor and as a facilitator

of yoga and dance. I teach my clients how to use their own breath to benefit their health and well-being. They often describe breathwork as a gateway to healing that they had yet to explore. Some people are hesitant to try deep, mindful breathing at first—they may think that it's stupid or they may have had negative experiences in previous attempts at practices like yoga or guided meditation. Others have to be gently guided to breathwork because the prospect of getting too relaxed is scary. But once we address any initial resistance and the mindful breathing begins to flow, I start witnessing small miracles on the quest toward wellness. When people get to know their breath, they are better able to scan their physical body and respond to what the body is asking for, whether it be sleep, stress relief, or the need for healthier food.

Commitment to deep, mindful breathing can lead to easier identification and management of difficult emotions. Our breath, like the wind passing through a sail, allows us to navigate potentially treacherous emotional terrain. Being able to breathe with whatever may rise up—anger, fear, grief, shame, or any number of other complex feelings—makes way for the practice of self-compassion. Intricately related to the mindfulness attitude of nonjudgment, self-compassion helps us respond to whatever may surface in all areas of life. The practice of self-compassion allows us to dig deeply and work to heal the old wounds that keep us from moving forward in the lives we want for ourselves. Ultimately, self-compassion empowers our own growth and personal transformation.

Breath as Sacred Life Force

In cultivating a connection to breath, we can more effectively tap into the voice of our inner self to discover what our spirit needs. Companionship, solitude, or loving-kindness are all examples of what may be revealed. The major faith traditions of the world all venerate breath's sacred, healing power in their sacred texts. Muslims believe that we breathe in the whole universe in each breath (Qur'an 6:156; 16:40). In his analysis of these Qur'anic passages and the writings of Sufi mystic Ibn 'Arabi, translator William Chittick observes, "God articulates each creature as a 'word' in his own breath, so the underlying substance of each thing is breath."[2]

The Muslim-born poet Kabir, whose writings influenced the development of the Bhakti movement within Hinduism, elegantly expressed this vital belief:

> Kabir says: Student, what is God?
> He is the breath inside the breath.[3]

The Chandogya Upanishad (5, 1, 1) describes *prana* (breath) as the oldest and greatest element of living. A poetry unfolds throughout this section to explain that even when other functions of life may fail—sight, speech, hearing, thought—the breath remains. In referencing each organ of the human body, the sacred text proclaims that "The *prana* alone is all of these." Buddhist texts spanning a period of over two thousand years are filled with teachings on the mindfulness of breath, with the Anapanasati Sutra providing the most specific instructions on breathing meditation. A passage from Theregata, a Buddhist scripture from the Pitaka Sutra translated as "verses of the elder monks," encapsulates the importance of mindful breathing in Buddhist practice:

> *One who has gradually practiced,*
> *Developed and brought to perfection*
> *Mindfulness of the in-and-out breath*
> *As taught by the Enlightened One*
> *Illuminates the entire world*
> *Like the moon when freed from the clouds.* (548)

Various writings in the Taoist tradition also convey a similarly lyrical reverence for the power of simple breathing. Ch'en Hsu-pai, as translated by Thomas Cleary, noted, "Breathing out and breathing in without interruption, the complete embryo forms and combines with the original beginning."[4] The theme of breath as rebirth radiates throughout Taoist texts.

The Judeo-Christian tradition also speaks to the life force that is breath. Growing up in this tradition, I heard the phrase *breath of life*, originating with the creation story in Genesis, with great regularity. In the gospel of John (20:22), Jesus appeared to his apostles after the resurrection and breathed on them, birthing the new church—the new Adam—into existence. Many scripture references from both the Hebrew Bible and the Christian Scriptures describe breath as a gift from God. The book of Job contains several passages specifically referencing breath as both a divine gift and a creative force (4:9; 12:10; 27:3; 33:4). Meditation scholar George Burke (Swami Nirmalanda Giri)[5] explains that in the Jewish tradition, meditation on the breath is a direct meditation on God.

Although all these passages speak to me, I am especially moved by the idea of breathing something into existence. That something doesn't have to be at the level of the new church, as Christ breathed; it can be as simple as breath giving life to the present moment. We can give breath to new connections, to new ideas. All innovation and creation is born of breath.

The words from Swami Svātmārāma's fifteenth-century manual on Hatha Yoga, which open this chapter, are often attributed to B.K.S. Iyengar (1918–2014), one of the major forces in bringing yoga to the West. In his classic book *Light on Yoga*, he wrote, "The mind is king of the senses, and the breath is the king of the mind." Reading Iyengar brought this idea to my attention several years before I set out on my own creative path of dancing mindfulness. Iyengar's presentation on the sutras and texts from the yogic traditions inspired me to incorporate breath more fully into my spiritual practices and in all areas of my life.

Not only do these teachings help me when I dance, but they also carry special meaning to me in my counseling work with others. Like most psychotherapists in the modern era, I received my training solely in the cognitive-behavioral paradigm. Cognitive-behavioral therapy holds that if people can change their thoughts, they can change their behaviors. However, many of us encounter limitations with this approach because the part of the brain that is affected by trauma and body-level stress has nothing to do with rational thought. I've personally and professionally witnessed how the gift of deep breathing can help us access those areas of the brain that need the most healing. These areas of the brain deal with emotion and body processes, not words and rational thought. One of my first yoga teachers slightly reworded Iyengar's quote as follows: "The mind controls the body, but the breath controls the mind." Upon hearing that, it clicked that it is not sufficient to just change our thinking to experience behavioral shifts. Rather, we must first change our breath, which can alter our thinking, positively impacting our behavior.

Martha Graham (1894–1991), the mother of contemporary dance, possessed a clear understanding about the impact of breath on motion. Many present-day teachers of conscious dance look to Martha Graham as a role model. Her inspirational sayings, such as "Dance is the hidden language of the soul," are often published as inspirational memes on social media. Promotional advertisements for dance classes and workshops also make use of them. After seeing so many Martha Graham quotes used in this way, I decided to go directly to the source and read her autobiography to discover what else she had to teach me. Aptly titled *Blood Memory*, Graham's autobiography is a fascinating study in holistic living. Her teaching on the breath brought tears to my eyes when I first read it, and I strive to convey the spirit of her message as I share the practice of dancing mindfulness with others:

> Every time you breathe life in or expel it, it is a release or a contraction. It is that basic to the body. You are born with these two movements and you keep both until you die. But you begin to use them consciously so that they are beneficial to the dance dramatically. You must animate that energy within yourself. Energy is that thing that sustains the world and the

universe. It animates the world and everything in it. I recognized early in my life that there was this kind of energy, some animating spark, or whatever you choose to call it. It can be Buddha, it can be anything, it can be everything. It begins with the breath.[6]

Using Graham's wisdom as inspiration, you can practice dancing mindfulness even if breath is the only element you choose to activate. Breath is life, dancing through us.

Setting Sail with Personal Practice

I usually begin dancing mindfulness practice in silence with three minutes or longer of a concentrated breath awareness exercise. Deep, mindful breathing stimulates the parasympathetic nervous system, essentially flipping your fight-flight-freeze reaction on its head. By deep breathing you are instead signaling your body to enter rest mode, and in this slower, nonreactionary state your ability to notice what's in the moment becomes more acute. Mindfulness is a practice of responding instead of reacting to stress, and the breath allows for this responsiveness. Listening to your breath provides you with critical information that can keep you safe during your dancing mindfulness practice. For instance, if you notice that you are becoming short of breath, it may be a sign that you've pushed yourself too far, physically or emotionally. In conventional exercise forms, we might say that this is a place to catch your breath. In dancing mindfulness practice, I like to say that these are moments to get reacquainted with your breath. By checking in with our breath in this way, our body will let us know if we need to rest in stillness or if, supported by our breath, we are able to keep moving in our dance.

How you ultimately choose to incorporate breath awareness strategies into your *Dancing Mindfulness* classes or personal dancing mindfulness practice is up to you. As you experiment with the practices provided here, feel free to modify them and make them your own; make the adjustments you need that help you connect with your breath. In doing so, may you become acquainted with the dance of your breath, and allow the breath to nourish your dance.

It Begins with Three

Many of the great writers on integrative medicine, including popular holistic personality Andrew Weil, MD, suggest that if a person can breathe mindfully, starting with three minutes each day, benefits will inevitably result. According to Weil, these benefits include more energy, a greater sense of calmness, and aid in healing stress-related health problems, like panic attacks and digestive disorders. In my years of counseling, teaching, and facilitating, I've discovered that three minutes is an excellent starting point for most people. Your mind may start to wander or drift off, and that is okay; beginning a mindfulness practice is about just that, *practicing* the art of coming back to the breath and learning that you can always come back to the breath.

I ease myself into personal practice with a brief breath awareness exercise and meditation. This breath-intensive warm-up is a key feature distinguishing dancing mindfulness from other, more workout-oriented dance forms. I recently attended a fitness-based class where the instructor's entire opening statement was on the importance of isolating the core muscles throughout the class so as to obtain bigger, more powerful movements. Indeed, the concept of core muscle isolation, which is essentially the societal message of "sucking it in," is what many conventionally trained dancers are taught. Dancing mindfulness is about going with the breath and letting the breath guide the movement. By staying true to what the breath reveals in its large, numinous waves, the movements may not be big and powerful, but they will be authentic.

Try This: Getting to Know Your Breath

- Begin in a comfortable, seated position. Focus on elongating your spine and avoid forcing any movements—think of sitting in a position that, for you, represents awareness.

- Just take a few moments to notice the natural rhythm of your breath. You don't have to do anything special, just notice. Be a witness, not a judge. If your mind starts to wander, that is okay. Know that you can always come back to the breath.

- After you've spent some time with your natural breath, I invite you to take your breath potential a little deeper. If you choose, you can bring one hand to your stomach area to further pay attention to your "belly breathing." On your next inhale, I invite you to consciously deepen the breath, feeling your stomach area fully expand to help you deepen the inhale.

- On the exhale, let the breath exit your mouth slowly and naturally as you notice the stomach draw back in. If it feels more natural to exhale through your nose, that is an appropriate modification. Another modification is to purposefully pucker your mouth—this allows you to slow down and notice the flow of the exhale.

- Once again, inhale with your nose and notice the belly expand, helping you to deepen your breath. Exhale with your mouth, as your belly pulls back in. Try several of these at your own pace.

- Continue noticing your breath, only now start tuning in to every little detail that you can. What sound does your breath make as your body forms and releases each breath? How does the breath feel in your body? Perhaps the breath even has a taste or a smell to it. Regard your breath as your body's own guide.

- Wherever else you may go with your dancing mindfulness practice on any given day, continue with this mindful breathing, even if you start to move your body in a more dynamic way. The breath will always tell you exactly what you need to know about yourself and your experience.

Finding Your Comfort Zone, and Moving Beyond It

As a practitioner of dancing mindfulness, you likely fall into one of two boats: either you love to dance so much the thought of slowing down to focus on your breath repulses you, or you are comfortable doing breathwork but you feel self-conscious about dancing. Think about which statement best describes you. Begin with where you are at, and then practice sailing the boat that is the greatest departure from your comfort zone as your practice deepens.

Let's start with the first situation: you love to dance but slowing down to relax and breathe unnerves you. In your own space, cue some music that speaks to you and dance with abandon. So much of dancing mindfulness draws on the joy of simply turning on the music and dancing around the house, so go ahead and do that! Whenever possible, be aware of your breath as you dance, paying special attention to deepening your breath to give you more energy as you move. When the song is over, come to a place of stillness; you can be standing, kneeling, in a lunge, or sitting, wherever the dance brings you at the end. Consider the term *stillness*. In the stillness just notice your breathing, nonjudgmentally, and pay attention to the process of allowing your breath to slow its pace over a period of time. This period is a perfect opportunity to also notice any of the attitudes of mindfulness that reveal themselves in that stillness:

- What is my breath teaching me about not judging myself so harshly?

- What is this experience of coming to stillness in my breath teaching me about trusting the process and not obsessing about outcomes?

- What may be keeping me from letting go of the need to control and just listening to my breath?

These questions are simply examples of what has come up for me during this practice—your experience may be different and totally organic to you. Whatever surfaces, I invite you to just cradle it in your awareness. From that point, notice if the practice prompts you toward further stillness or toward an enhanced appreciation of the mindfulness of your movement.

In the second scenario, let's say you are the type who gets freaked out by dancing or moving, especially out of fear that others are judging you. Maybe when you try to move freely, your own inner critic begins to chatter—for many of us, that's the worst judge of all! Begin with a breath practice of your choice, using the "Getting to Know Your Breath" practice (page 7) if you need some guidance. After you've noticed your breathing begin to deepen and lengthen, think about the breath moving first to your arms. As you inhale, begin to move your arms in a way that feels right for you. You may draw inspiration from calling to mind an image that works for you, like palm trees swaying in the breeze or the arms of a mythical creature moving in a celestial trance. If it helps, imagine that your breath has a color or a mix of colors—perhaps you are breathing in a swirl of blue, purple, and rose. Imagine the breath sending those colors to your arms, inspiring movement. Let the breath do the work. You might want to think about your breath as channeling the Divine. Then simply notice what happens.

In addition to practicing nonjudgment, this experience is a perfect opportunity to practice the attitude of beginner's mind. Beginner's mind challenges us to set aside any preconceived judgments or expectations about what should be happening and engage in an activity as if we're doing it for the first time. Let the breath move your arms as a child might move his—uninhibited by self-criticism or judgment on how things *should* look. In doing so, a sense of wonder and curiosity may rise up within you. If that happens, play with it for a while. After you move your arms, see where your breath goes next and continue with this pattern of experimental movement. If you want to do this in silence, you may. If listening to music helps you, go ahead and cue some up for this practice. Wherever this particular practice may take you, let your breath guide the process.

In my personal dancing mindfulness practice, I work with the idea of "breathing in" the music. I invite myself to breathe in the sound that I'm hearing, and when I facilitate classes I invite my participants to do the same. This esoteric invitation may sound like a completely foreign idea. Sometimes I am met with stares, suggesting, "What do you mean *breathe in* the music?" If you can ponder the idea for a moment, see if it offers another channel for you to work with the element of breath. Along with the heartbeat, breath offers a natural rhythm that, together with music, can guide you to deeper levels of awareness in your body and on your emotional journey. In personal practice, call upon this idea of "breathing in" sound whenever it feels right to do so, or if you need some inspiration. The following chapter on sound will hopefully foster even more ideas on how you can fuse breath and sound in your personal practice.

Try This: Breathing in the Music

- Bring your hand to your heart.

- As you hear the first tones of music, specifically draw your awareness to your breath.

- Remember that breathing is a sacred act, your breath is a channel, sending information from your soul to your body.

- Let the tones of the music blend with your breath.

- Allow your breath to translate the message that your spirit wishes to send to your body.

- Notice what happens, refraining from judging or anticipating. Simply be present to how this practice unfolds.

From Jamie's Music Box:
Top Picks for Breathing in the Music

Here are some of my personal favorite pieces for "breathing in the music" in my dancing mindfulness practice. If these don't work for you, keep in mind that there is no "wrong" music in dancing mindfulness practice. Just experiment with what helps you best connect to the practice. I find experimentation to be a fun part of the process.

- "The Feeling Begins" (Peter Gabriel)

- Theme from *The Mission* (Ennio Morricone)

- "Om" (Soulfood)

- "The Morning Room" (Helios)

- "Ubi Caritas" (Gregorian chant)

- "The Wind" (Cat Stevens/Yusuf Islam)

- "Iguazu" from the *Babel* soundtrack (Gustavo Santaollala); soundtracks are a good place to find similar types of music

- Gentle instrumental versions of Celtic folk songs, such as "Wild Mountain Thyme," "Fields of Athenry," or "Danny Boy"; American folk songs, such as "Simple Gifts," can be lovely, as well as certain versions of folk songs from any global tradition. I strongly resonate with traditional Chinese music for this practice.

- "Thaïs: Meditation" (Jules Massenet) and similar classical pieces that make gentle yet emotionally evocative use of pianos and/or violins; "Für Elise" (Ludwig van Beethoven) is another solid option in this vein.

Resting with the Breath

In my personal dancing mindful practice, I wind down the class with a classic, yogic *sivasana*, or relaxation period. *Sivasana*, or corpse pose, is exactly what the name suggests. In this practice you return to the ground, lying flat on your back (if physically possible), with palms up and, if comfortable, eyes closed. Although the term *corpse* is morbid to some, I have always embraced the "deathly" connotation of that word to mean surrender, as opposed to actual death. *Sivasana* typically offers me an opportunity to revisit the breath in this position of profound connection to the earth. I often thank my breath for guiding me through my practice that day. When I am in *sivasana*, I sometimes contemplate the death of my old unhealthy ways of being so that I can more fully embrace my newfound connection to the earth, my body, and, of course, my breath. Other times my practice of *sivasana* takes me to a place of simple, pure being—I think of nothing, and that's the beauty of it!

Launching Out: Sharing the Practice with Others and Deepening Your Personal Practice

If you are responding to an inner prompting to share the dancing mindfulness practice with others, the practices covered in this chapter are appropriate for group facilitation. I routinely use "Getting to Know Your Breath" and "Breathing in the Music" in *Dancing Mindfulness* classes; the key is modifying each practice to the respective groups. For instance, if you notice that three minutes is either too long or not long enough in "Getting to Know Your Breath," you are free to alter the time that you spend in this practice. I strongly suggest that you work in this breath awareness exercise at some point during the practice, usually the beginning. The only exception I make to that suggestion is if you are working with a group that, overall, may seem too fidgety to even settle down to breathe. If that's the case, consider beginning with free-form movement and then working to a place of stillness.

Another major example of modification can occur during the *sivasana* period at the end of practice. You may not want to facilitate a *sivasana* in a traditional, yogic sense by having everyone lie down on the floor. In fact, if you feel that doing so leaves your group feeling emotionally vulnerable, you may have everyone end in a seated posture instead. Because of health issues, some participants are not able to lie flat on the floor. Thus, even if you are offering a classic *sivasana*, consider giving people the option of lying down, sitting on the floor (perhaps against a wall for extra support), or returning to a chair. I provide more suggestions on facilitating an amazing *sivasana* experience for your group as we visit the other elements in the chapters to follow. As it relates to the element of breath covered in this chapter, ask yourself this question: Is the way I'm setting up the *sivasana* experience at the end of a group practice optimally conducive for helping people reconnect with their breath?

Just Checking In

As a facilitator, I consider it a privilege to remind people to notice their breath throughout the practice, not just during the opening meditation or the closing *sivasana*. When I open a group experience, I let participants know that we will be "checking in" with the breath several times throughout the practice. *Checking in* simply means to notice and then make adjustments or modifications based on what people may discover by listening to the breath. I also advise my participants that even if I don't directly say it, they can check in with their breath at any time during the practice. In my experience, people can benefit from this "check-in" practice if they are feeling lost in a dance or uncomfortable with a certain risk the dance is asking them to take, or if their body simply needs a break.

If you're facilitating a class, your participants would obviously be annoyed if, every two minutes, you invited them to "check in with" or "notice" the breath. As with all great facilitation techniques, they have to be well placed, well timed, and properly balanced. Since I am more of a go-with-the-flow style of facilitator, I rarely plan when I'm going to do breath check-ins. I find that in a standard, hour-long class, I typically make at least an invitation every other song. Statements that I often use include:

- Remember to check in with your breath.

- Notice your breath. What is your breath telling you right now?

- Let your breathing guide your movement.

- It's important for you to continue to breathe, even when we increase the tempo.

- Know that you can always come back to the breath; your breath will tell you exactly what's going on.

- Notice what effect the music is having on your breath.

- Be aware of your breath; allow your breath to help you relax or soften.

- As you check in with your breath, thank your breath for guiding you through your practice today.

- Allow your breath to help the old fall away. Allow your breath to let the new enter in.

- Be sure to check in with your breath now that you've returned to the earth.

This practice of checking in with the breath may apply to you as you deepen your personal practice as well as in your facilitation. You may struggle with actively drawing your awareness to the breath, especially as the pace of your dance picks up. It's easy to neglect the practice of consciously noticing an element like breath unless someone is there to remind us. If you know that you struggle with breathing during personal practice, consider writing some of these facilitator statements down on sticky notes and placing them around the space where you dance mindfully. I've actively practiced dancing mindfulness for many years and I still consult my sticky notes from time to time.

These are just suggestions. Be creative and true to your authentic self as a facilitator or in your personal practice. If you are facilitating, consider what breath awareness has meant to you in your various practices, such as meditation, yoga, dance, or other spiritually creative pursuits. Share some of this personal meaning with others in the group. The best facilitation prompts flow from your own experience. Let your own relationship with your breath nurture this sense of natural flow. Perhaps you entered a special place emotionally or spiritually as you facilitated a class. Another tip I can pass along is to take a moment during one of the silent periods in *sivasana* and really savor it. Take a deep breath yourself. Have your own special breath check-in, and any words you may require to close the class will come to you naturally.

Weaving It All Together

A dancing mindfulness practitioner once shared something about breath that brought a huge smile to my face. This lady regularly attends community practice, and she also dances in other venues, including ballrooms and clubs. She made an observation about how one of her friends dances: "This girl is a wonderful dancer, but she forgets to breathe when she dances. She always forgets to breathe. And I'm afraid she's going to hurt herself." Her reflection didn't seem nasty or judgmental, and I pursued the conversation further. The more we talked, the more we marveled at how remembering to breathe mindfully enhances the overall experience of dance. We both agreed that mindful breathing keeps us safe by telling us when we may need a break and nourishing our bodies during periods of dynamic movement. When I move together with deep breath, I consistently experience a greater sense of presence with the dance, and I find that my other senses are heightened, too. In other words, breathing consciously can help us to better savor the experience of dancing. For participants in dancing mindfulness, this idea hopefully translates into savoring life.

In his book *A Lion Among Men* (number three in the series that became the hit musical *Wicked*), Gregory Maguire expresses through the character Sister Doctor: "Remember to breathe. It is, after all, the secret of life."[7] Through my journey of deepening my own personal practice and sharing it with others, I can accept the full beauty of this teaching. My breath, my life, and my dance are all one. They are connected like their own version of the holy Trinity, sustaining each other, flourishing because of each other.

I hope the suggestions offered in this chapter give you some ideas about where to start with your own dancing mindfulness practice. If you already engage in dancing mindfulness, it is my wish that revisiting some of the ideas in this chapter will help you deepen your practice. Experiment, explore, be curious. Enter the practices from a place of beginner's mind—as if you were new to this world and trying them each for the first time. May you find the breath anew in each practice. Intoning the words of Martha Graham once again, it all begins with the breath.

Try This: Breath, the Seven Attitudes, and the Creative Arts

If you are breathing, you are dancing.

Are you allowing breath and dance to learn from each other?

Are you open to what they can teach you about living?

- Consider the seven foundational attitudes of mindfulness practice: nonjudging, patience, beginner's mind, trust, nonstriving, acceptance, letting go.

- How does each attitude relate to breath? Consider assigning a physical movement or gesture to each attitude and see what happens with your breath when you do that.

- How can the practice of breath, especially in concert with movement, help you to further develop these seven attitudes for your optimal health and well-being?

I encourage you to use dance, or any of the other creative arts, to contemplate these questions—get out your journal, your paints, your pencils, your camera—whatever helps you enter this place of contemplation. Perhaps you are a songwriter, a poet, or a fiction writer. Consider these channels to help you dance with the questions. Notice the connections that rise up when you fuse the practice of dancing mindfulness together with any of your other practices or creative pursuits.

Other Voices on Breath

Burke, George (Swami Nirmalanda Giri). *Learn How to Meditate: Breath Meditation*. Cedar Crest, NM: Light of the Spirit Monastery. Available online at www.breathmeditation.org.

Graham, Martha. *Blood Memory: An Autobiography*. New York: Doubleday, 1991.

Hanh, Thich Nhat. *Breathe! You Are Alive: Sutra on the Awareness of Breathing*. Berkeley, CA: Parallax Press, 2008.

Iyengar, B.K.S., and Yehudi Menuhim. *Light on Pranayama: The Art of Yogic Breathing*. New York: The Crossroad Publishing Company, 1985.

Kabat-Zinn, Jon. *Full Catastrophe Living: Using the Wisdom of Your Body and Mind to Face Stress, Pain, and Illness*. New York: Bantam Dell, 1990.

Weintraub, Amy. *Yoga Skills for Therapists: Effective Practices for Mood Management*. New York: W.W. Norton & Co., 2012.

Chapter 2

Sound

Attunement to the Process of Living

And those who were seen dancing were thought to be insane
by those who could not hear the music.

—*Friedrich Nietzsche*

Right around the time that I was conceived, a Canadian musician named Frank Mills released an unlikely hit single, a piano instrumental called "Music Box Dancer." My mother fell in love with the song immediately and played the record for me while I was in her womb. She even learned to play it on the piano herself. Regardless of where I am or how I hear it, the song evokes a strong emotional response in me, a feeling of connection to the cosmos. Also in the late 1970s, as the disco craze swept the nation, my mother—yes, the same woman—took disco dancing lessons and she continued while she was pregnant with me. To this day, my friends tease me about my love of the Swedish supergroup ABBA, and I cite as the reason my in

19

utero exposure to their music, sealed by my mother's rhythmic dance moves. I bawled when I saw the stage version and the movie version of *Mamma Mia!* and I even sang "Thank You for the Music" in tribute to my mother at her retirement party. As strange as it sounds, ABBA, the first group of musicians on the soundtrack of my life, always has a perfect song in their catalog to help me define exactly what I'm feeling at any given time. Perhaps it is not so strange if you comprehend the magical hold music can have on a person, even if it is the music of cheesy Swedish megapop!

As the Russian novelist Leo Tolstoy noted, "Music is the shorthand of emotion." Music, a celebrated manifestation of sound in cultures around the planet, is linked with so many emotions in human beings, whether those emotions are celebratory or solemn. We tend to associate certain pieces of music with memories or times in our life, and sometimes revisiting these songs is the best way to work through emotional blockages. The playwright and poet Oscar Wilde realized this phenomenon when he described music as "the art that is most nigh to tears and memory."

I've always been a lover of music. Although I can sing and play musical instruments, I tend to have an even deeper experience when I'm listening to it. When I figure-skated, one of my favorite things to do was select music to accompany my routines. So often I would cue up music in my bedroom or in the basement and choreograph programs I would never have the technical prowess to skate to, but I would live the program in my head or dance what I could of it in the house. I engaged in this practice regularly in my early adolescence. I was dealing with bullying from my peers and drama in my parents' marriage, and many days I felt emotionally suffocated both at school and at home. Being able to create my own adventures, fueled by the power of music, was incredibly healing. This practice allowed me to exercise acceptance and patience, and it gave me an outlet for coping with—or, in my case, dancing through—a very stressful season of my life.

Some of my favorite writers serve as prolific teachers on weaving music into the healing process. The poet and novelist Maya Angelou directly credits the power of music as a healing vehicle in her auto-biographical *Gather Together in My Name* (1974). She recalls: "Music was my refuge. I could crawl into the space between the notes and curl my back to loneliness."[1] *Gather Together in My Name* chronicles a period of Angelou's life from the ages of seventeen to nineteen when she struggled to make ends meet as a single mother, often resorting to trading sex for money. Angelou's explanation of music as a way to ease her loneliness parallels the sentiment of legendary poet Robert Browning: "He who hears music, feels his solitude peopled at once."

What Is Music?

Let's explore what music actually means by examining various per-spectives from global traditions. I have always seen music, like mind-fulness, as something that you need to experience—you don't get the full effect by just reading about it or talking about it. Nonetheless, writers continue their attempts to find just the right combination of words to offer a workable definition:

- **Random House dictionary (first definition):** an art of sound in time that expresses ideas and emotions in significant forms through the elements of rhythm, melody, harmony, and color.

- **Wikipedia (Let's face it, you go there too for the instant "lookup"):** an art form whose medium is sound and silence. Common elements of music are pitch, rhythm, dynamics, and the sonic qualities of timbre and texture.

- **Etymological (word) origin from *A Greek-English Lexicon*:** from the Greek, *mousike techne*, meaning "art of the muses." Another Greek derivation is *mousikos*, meaning "of or pertaining to the muses." According to a Greek myth, one of the lesser-known goddesses, Voce, created the world by singing it into existence.[2]

Music is a vital force in the lifeblood of Native American spirituality. Priscilla Coolidge, a member of the Cherokee nation and a founding member of the musical group Walela, proclaims:

Our music then became a promise to our grandmother to keep the stories alive.... Our music was born out of a vision by our grandmother. There was so much repression for some of our elders during those dark years when songs couldn't be sung and ceremonies were out of the question.[3]

Musician and music scholar Douglas Spotted Eagle explains that Native Americans view music as the heartbeat of Mother Earth:

From the time that our early ancestors began to communicate with the earth, through the use of drums, to the time that the flute was given to the people, the music has been a major participant in both ceremony and daily life.[4]

Singer-songwriter Joey Weisenberg makes similar observations about the role of listening and music in Jewish life. In an interview Weisenberg gave about music as a spiritual practice, he observed:

Music teaches us how to *listen*—if we let it. It is through careful listening that we learn how to get "in tune" with the people, spaces, and spiritual energies around us ... It is through intentional listening, our tradition teaches, that we are able to close our eyes and better hear the unity that underlies all of creation.... When our hearts are opened through music, we are more vulnerable, but we are also more receptive to insight.[5]

Weisenberg's presentation of this tradition bears many similarities to the meaning behind *Om*, the chant tone representing the convergence of all the vibrations of the universe. Originating in Hindu tradition, the symbol and ideas of this chant tone are also applied in Buddhism, Jainism, and Sikhism. *Om* is well known by many Westerners who attend yoga and meditation classes, as chanting this vibration has become a customary way to end classes. The meaning behind the chant is incredibly profound and can provide us with a beautiful way to tap into the energy of the universe through the portal of sound.

Hazrat Inayat Khan extolled the virtues of sound as universal vibration. Khan was the founder of the Sufi Order of the West and a classically trained musician in the northern Indian tradition. In the second volume of his series on Sufi teachings, Khan expounds on the role that music plays in universal life:

> Music is a miniature of the harmony of the whole universe, for the harmony of the universe is life itself, and humans, being a miniature of the universe, show harmonious and inharmonious chords in their pulsations, in the beat of their hearts, in their vibration, rhythm and tone. Their health or illness, their joy or discomfort, all show the music or lack of music in their life. And what does music teach us? Music helps us to train ourselves in harmony, and it is this which is the magic or the secret behind music. When you hear music that you enjoy, it tunes you and puts you in harmony with life.[6]

African tradition is also filled with a collection of proverbs casting music as a metaphor for life, with various proverbs specifically addressing the convergence of music and dance as representative of the life experience. Just consider this small sampling:

- He who understands music understands the cosmos. (Egyptian)

- If the rhythm of the drumbeat changes, the dance steps must also adapt. (Kossi)

- When the music changes, then the rhythm of the dance must change also. (Tuareg)

- When the music changes so does the dance. (Nigerian)

- Move your neck according to the music. (Ethiopian)

- In a fiddler's house, all are dancers. (Rwandan)

When I meditate on these proverbs, I feel a sense of ancient wisdom validating what I realized for myself about dance and music growing up in the Christian tradition.

Even when I felt misunderstood, judged, or disconnected in services at both Christian denominations of my youth, the music never failed to speak to me. Singing along in both the Catholic Mass (my mom's tradition) and Evangelical services (my dad's adopted path) proved to be the most powerful vehicle for my prayer. To this day, when I sing I communicate with the Divine. That song might be a traditional Gregorian chant, a modern hymn, a piece of contemporary praise music, or a pop hit that holds spiritual meaning for me. I still find myself dancing around the house to music I once heard as a child back in church if am so moved by spirit. It's no wonder that one of my favorite psalms in Scripture is Psalm 98; verses 4–7 are especially powerful and echo the wisdom found in many of the traditions already presented in this chapter:

> Shout for joy to the LORD, all the earth,
>   burst into jubilant song with music;
> make music to the LORD with the harp,
>   with the harp and the sound of singing,
> with trumpets and the blast of the ram's horn—
>   shout for joy before the LORD, the King.
>
> Let the sea resound, and everything in it,
>   the world, and all who live in it.
> Let the rivers clap their hands,
>   let the mountains sing together for joy;
>   let them sing before the Lord,
>   for he comes to judge the earth.
> He will judge the world in righteousness
>   and the peoples with equity.

Not only do I adore this explanation of God's judgment as something that is righteous and equitable (as opposed to something scary and daunting), but I am also moved by the nature imagery. *The rivers clapping their hands* is an especially joyous description of nature's song, reminding me that in dancing mindfulness practice, the sounds of nature often provide the best accompaniment.

How we experience and even define music is subjective; it's different for everyone. Neuroscientist and music scholar Daniel J. Levitin, author of *This Is Your Brain on Music,* elaborates:

> What is music? To many, "music" can only mean the great masters—Beethoven, Debussy, and Mozart. To others, "music" is Busta Rhymes, Dr. Dre, and Moby. To one of my saxophone teachers at Berklee College of Music—and to legions of "traditional jazz" aficionados—anything made before 1940 or after 1960 isn't *really* music at all.[7]

Interestingly, in both my personal dancing mindfulness practice and in classes, I try to include a plethora of genres. And yes, I've used Claude Debussy and Dr. Dre in the same class! As we set sail with personal practice using the element of sound, I ask you to honor what music teaches you about your practice, yourself, and life in general. Additionally, I challenge you to approach this element of the practice with a sense of curiosity and beginner's mind—in other words, be willing to listen outside of your comfort zone. Notice if different sounds or styles of music speak to you throughout the process. Your tastes might lean toward Debussy, but are you open to what Dr. Dre can teach you?

Setting Sail with Personal Practice

Musical connection is one of the most vital elements of my personal dancing mindfulness practice. I am a musician, and taking refuge in music brought solace during my childhood. Thus, the opportunities for musical exploration in the practice may be more important for me than they are for you. That's okay—variations and modifications are celebrated in dancing mindfulness. In cultivating your dancing mindfulness practice, you may discover that simple sounds have a greater impact for you. You may never have to fire up the CD player or iPod. Community *Dancing Mindfulness* classes often draw avid drum circle enthusiasts and facilitators. When these participants attend classes, I always notice how they slap their hands against their legs to generate sound. This experience is a key part of connecting to the practice for them. I avidly encourage making your own percussion in dancing mindfulness practice. Stomping my feet on the ground and just going with that sound is one of my favorite maneuvers!

In my personal practice and in my classes, sound is the next element I focus on after breath. There are multiple connections we can make between breath and sound. Your breath is an instrument and this is especially apparent when you let your breath make a sound. Go ahead and try it. Inhale and when you exhale, make the exhale audible. Let the sound of your exhale—whether it be a sigh, a grunt, or some unique sound that can't easily be described in words—help you let go of anything you're holding that no longer serves you. For example, we can use the audible exhale to help us let go of stress, tension, anxiety, or fixation on an outcome.

Try This: Ocean-Sounding Victory Breath

When practicing a dynamic yogic breath technique like ocean-sounding victory breath (*ujjayi* breathing in Sanskrit), the quality of sound in your breath is obvious. Some people refer to this as Darth Vader breathing—referencing the character from *Star Wars* films. You can use his deep respiration as an inspiration for helping you generate sound. Here are some guidelines if you want to give this technique a try:

- Pucker your mouth like you're sucking through a straw or about to kiss someone. This pucker creates a slight contraction in the back of your throat, which helps to produce more sound.

- Inhale through your nose, allowing your belly to expand with this motion.

- Exhale through your nose; although air may flow out of your mouth, think about doing the work with your nose.

- If your mouth is puckered and your throat is contracted, you ought to hear the sound of the ocean within you. Don't be afraid to use your breath to help you get loud.

- Attempt to keep the inhales and exhales even, especially while you're first learning this breathing technique—this helps to prevent uncomfortable lightheadedness.

Practice Note

Do not attempt more than five full sets during your first pass if you are new to this breathing technique. It is completely normal if you feel somewhat lightheaded, but it ought to be a positive sensation. If it does not feel good, chances are you tried too many too soon, or the inhales and exhales were uneven. If you struggle with respiratory problems, you are prone to fainting, or you are pregnant, avoid doing this breath at full force; try it gently at first to see how you respond before taking it further. For a video demonstration of this breathing technique, visit the *Dancing Mindfulness* resource page at www.dancingmindfulness.com/resources.

Breath practice, especially more physically vigorous breaths like *ujjayi* breathing, can create noticeable vibrations in the body. Sonic vibration produces energy; that is why individuals who are hearing impaired may enjoy listening to music. Vibration is the tactile element of sound, and it can take us places emotionally and viscerally. Our pulse creates this same vibration. Consider that your heartbeat is a rhythm that is always with you. Your heartbeat is built-in percussion. As with breath, you can always check in with or notice your heartbeat during dancing mindfulness practice. Listen to your heartbeat. What is it telling you? Maybe your heartbeat is telling you that it's time for a break, a pause in stillness. Your pumping heart may also reveal that movement feels good in the body. For me, a healthfully pumping heart during dancing mindfulness practice helps me tap into the energy I've stirred up in my practice. I can listen to this energy, without judgment, and notice where my practice wants to take me next. Through dancing mindfulness practice, I've learned to trust my own heartbeat.

When you recognize that your heartbeat is your own natural musical instrument, there is so much you can do with this awareness. In addition to the physical information, I often ask these questions of my beating heart: What do you want me to know in this moment? Where do you want me to go next? Now imagine where you can go if you weave together your heartbeat, your intention for practice, and other sounds or pieces of music.

Try This: Mindful Listening, Mindful Movement

Too often music plays in the background, like elevator music. In this exercise, we will explore how paying attention to music in a nonjudgmental manner can usher in a new experience of listening to music. For optimal discovery, you are encouraged to try all four parts of this exercise, in order.

- Get into a comfortable yet alert position, as if you were about to do a sitting or lying-down meditation (your choice). Cue up a piece of music that you have never heard before (go on the Internet to find something or dig into the unpopular tracks of your CD/tape collection). For the length of the song, your only task is to pay attention to the song, listening mindfully. If you sense a desire to move, you don't have to suppress it, although I challenge you to restrict the experience to listening. We will be moving in the next part of the exercise.

- After a few minutes of silence, cue up the song again and let the music connect with your breath. Be open to movement, should it happen, and just go with it. You may only be inspired to sway and swivel a little bit, or you may break out into a full-on dance. Whatever happens, just honor the experience.

- Now find a piece of music that you know very well, preferably something that you connect with emotionally. Return to your sitting or lying meditative position and listen to this piece of music with total awareness, as if it's the first time you're hearing it. Approach this listening with a sense of beginner's mind. Once again, just be with the experience and notice what happens within you when you listen with mindful ears.

- Replay the song, this time being open to movement. Just go with it and notice what happens.

- If you are deeply engaged in this practice and wish to continue, put your iPod or MP3 player on shuffle and let the sweet randomness guide your practice. Continue with this pattern of listening first, then opening to movement when you replay the song.

Try This: Heart Choreography

Choreography is a planned series of steps and movements that dancers learn to create their performance. Since there are no planned steps in dancing mindfulness, I like to think of your personal choreography—the steps and movements you will take throughout your practice—as coming from the heart. You can do this practice after a period of stillness or after dancing to some music, as in the "Mindful Listening, Mindful Movement" exercise on page 28.

- Bring your dominant hand to your heart. Really feel the pulsation of your heartbeat with your hand, and notice the energy from those vibrations moving into the rest of your body.

- Allow this energy to work into your other arm, and notice what happens to that arm. Think about your heart sending its sacred choreography into that other arm, and then into your whole body. Let this process unfold for at least one to two minutes, going longer if you are so moved.

- Transition to your nondominant hand, bringing that hand to your heart. Once again, notice the vibrational energy emanating from your heart, moving through your body. Just allow the natural dance of your heart to unfold, only now on this side. Go with it and notice what happens.

There are a variety of musical choices you can employ in the "Heart Choreography" practice. Perhaps what you discovered in the "Mindful Listening, Mindful Movement" practice will give you what you need. I generally use an instrumental, although certain songs with just the right lyrics about honoring yourself or listening to your heart may be appropriate (a song like Madonna's "Open Your Heart" comes to mind). You can also engage in the "Heart Choreography" practice in total silence. In both personal and group practice, I sometimes find that silence is the most profound and needed of all the sounds, a concept that singer-songwriter Paul Simon captured beautifully in his song "Sound of Silence." Sometimes I use Simon's classic to begin this "Heart Choreography" or a similar dance and then continue in total silence.

The Art of the Playlist

Whether you experience the healing power of sound through vibration or through music, the possibilities for expanding where you can go with mindful awareness are limitless. I cherish putting together playlists for *Dancing Mindfulness* classes or my own personal practice. This process allows me to listen to new material and call upon pieces of music that have resonated for me over the years. I have quite a collection on my computer, so mixing and matching is fun. Sometimes I get just as much insight or even healing from putting the playlist together as I do from dancing to it, a testament to music's healing power. Designing playlists is a practice that is made easier by modern technology. Programs like iTunes and Windows Media Player, and Internet services like Spotify, are examples of platforms that can assist you in this process. I've learned from training facilitators that there isn't a perfect platform for everyone. My best suggestion is to experiment and see which platform works best for you. If you are feeling lost in working with the technology, consider going to your local electronics store and enlisting tech support. We've come a long way from making mix tapes in the 1980s, and you can use this technology to enhance your practice.

I look at playlists as collages. When I design them for classes, I often have a theme in mind—one of the mindfulness attitudes, a season of the year, a theological concept, a decade—and build my musical selections from there. In making playlists for personal practice, I find I can go even deeper. For instance, if I am working through a period of grief or loss, I design my playlist with that in mind, helping me dance through the experience. If I'm celebrating good news, I craft a playlist that helps me express gratitude and joy specific to my celebration. Perhaps I am feeling a little distant from spirit. I often find that making a playlist with a spiritual theme, including songs that express my doubt and vulnerability, helps me reconnect.

From Jamie's Music Box:
Ideas for Playlists and Themes

I am a playlist pack rat! Once I make a playlist of music, I keep it, part for posterity and mostly because I may need to draw on similar inspiration later on. In this glimpse into my musical collection, I am sharing with you some of the playlist themes I've made for personal practice over the years:

- Celebrating the aspects of life that make me happy

- The interplay between darkness and light

- The yin/yang of saying yes and no

- Hymns and praise songs from my childhood

- Nature sounds and songs inspired by nature

- Nonstriving: giving myself permission to not try so hard

- Grieving the loss of a romantic relationship

- Grieving the loss of a deceased loved one

- Dancing the songs I'd like played at my funeral

- Connecting to the God of my understanding

- Tapping into my love for a TV show or movie by dancing the soundtrack

Hopefully, this list gives you some ideas to start making your own playlists for personal practice. Remember that playlists do not have to be any particular length. You may come up with three songs that perfectly reflect what you are going through at a given point in your life and this constitutes your sacred playlist for that personal practice.

Launching Out: Sharing the Practice with Others and Deepening Your Personal Practice

Because my tastes in music are so varied, it's easy for me to draw on a variety of genres when I share the dancing mindfulness practice with others. Musical variety also pays homage to the many ways that mindfulness can be practiced—opportunities for mindful practice exist in all areas of life. Similarly, there is a style of music to correspond with all the ways of being in the world. My musical collection spans decades, styles, and continents, so it is true to my genuine self to include multiple genres, as long as they fit together somehow for a given class. I also see this as a way of offering "something for everyone" in my classes. However, you do not have to follow this guidance. As I once told a facilitator I trained, you can have an acid rock–themed *Dancing Mindfulness* class, as long as the music leads the class in some positive, mindful direction and it resonates with the people in your class.

A regular participant in my classes once asked me to facilitate *Dancing Mindfulness* for a cancer support group she attended in our community. I seriously underestimated the median age of the class. When I arrived at the class I was pleasantly surprised to see that, with the exception of the woman who had invited me, the youngest person in the class was seventy. We modified the opening sequence to look more like chair yoga and I rearranged some songs on the fly that seemed to better fit the group. I worked some big band and "oldies" rock into the playlist and we had a blast! Of course, you are never going to please everyone in a class, but you must be attuned to the dynamics of your group when making musical selections.

It seems a bit silly to offer specific songs or pieces of music in this chapter, since the general idea here is that *all* music may work, depending on the class, the context, and the arrangement of each piece. My general guidance is to make sure that the music somehow ties in to the attitudes of mindfulness or general positivity and well-being. Don't get me wrong: sometimes I use dark songs (for example, "Mad World" by Tears for Fears, covered by many others), songs of loss ("Tennessee Waltz," various versions), angsty ballads ("Rolling in the Deep" by Adele), empowering rants ("Joy" by Lucinda Williams), and, on rare occasions if the class is right, something really angry ("Angry Chair" by Alice in Chains). However, when using this music, I attempt to elicit some grief or another dark emotion in order to work through those feelings. I strive to move people from this darker place to a place of healing and positivity.

Inspiring Transitions

There are many junctures for transition in a dancing mindfulness personal practice or group practice, and using just the right music can help participants experience shifting awareness. For instance, moving from a slower warm-up on the floor to moving onto the feet is a transition point. It's important to choose music that eases the transition.

One of my favorite facilitation strategies is to invite people to just naturally notice what happens in their body and in their dance when the song changes. For example, after the participants are on their feet, I like to play a song for exploring the space—for example, "Ornico Flow" by Enya, or the classic theme from *Zorba the Greek*. Then I simply invite them to notice what happens when the music shifts to something that is more high-energy. Latin music is a good source to draw from for this shift, or any pop song that elicits a "power walk" response. The Tina Turner classic "Proud Mary" is an ideal song for transition because it starts mellow and then, about halfway through, the beat drops and a bouncier, more dynamic vibe takes over.

Another choice to make in selecting music is whether to use songs with lyrics or instrumentals. I like to strike a balance in my personal practice and classes. Sometimes the lyrics are positive, meaningful, and powerful, and I encourage participants to really listen to what the lyrics are saying and allow the lyrics to help them create their dance. Classics like Michael Jackson's "Man in the Mirror" and hymns like "Wade in the Water" or "Amazing Grace" can work nicely for this facilitation. In my opinion, there is a place for lyrics and a place for instrumentals. Sometimes the lyrics may get in the way of emotional connection. I usually opt for an instrumental when I dance "Heart Choreography," both in my personal practice and when I share that practice with a group.

I've also learned that people have their own personal preferences about what works for them when it comes to lyrics versus no lyrics. My dear friend and colleague Dr. Paschal Baute, who, at eighty-five years young, regularly practices dancing mindfulness, prefers instrumentals. When we cofacilitated a workshop, he was annoyed that I used so many songs with lyrics; for him, lyrics get in the way of optimally connecting with his bodily experiences. Another time I challenged myself to put together an entire *Dancing Mindfulness* class playlist that was all instrumental. It seemed like a good idea, since the focus of the class was the sixth chakra, the energetic center of the forehead, associated with intuition, insight, and wisdom. I challenged people throughout the class to dance with their mental processes, free of interference from the lyrics. One regular community practitioner and now facilitator, Rachel Weaver (who loves lyrics), told me, "When I heard you were doing that [no lyrics] I almost didn't come. I wasn't sure how I was going to connect without lyrics." Fortunately, she and others kept an open mind to the process and that all-instrumental class remains one of my favorites. The challenge here is to be open to stepping out of your comfort zone. Personal practice allows us to engage with this challenge.

Try This: Share Your Music, Share the Practice

I offer you the following suggestions about selecting music for *Dancing Mindfulness* group practice, based on my own experience as a dancer and as a facilitator.

- Getting excited about music and knowing how it has the potential to move people are the keys to success in facilitating *Dancing Mindfulness*. You do not have to be a professional musician to tap into this power.

- Having a mastery of the MP3/iPod technology will make your life much easier when it comes to making playlists and being able to alter your music program on the fly during classes. If this is an area that you need to spend some time mastering, seek help from people you know or check out a local electronics store to see what is available by way of technical support.

- In constructing playlists, you'll get a sense of what kind of music will work for the classes where you are sharing the practice. In general, the songs that you like to dance to form a solid foundation; keep an open mind to music that you hear at other classes, in public, or by playlist sharing. The *Dancing Mindfulness* community forum on Facebook is a great place to share and swap ideas.

- Listen for the "grab" factor in music. If a song doesn't move you, chances are it will be a dud with the class. Just as with counseling or other areas of ministry, if you don't believe in what you're offering, the method will not likely be the best fit for the person or people you're serving.

- All types of music in every genre can work in *Dancing Mindfulness*. Strive to choose music that promotes the attitudes of mindfulness whenever possible, but don't feel that each song has to pass a test. Be sure to listen to your lyrics and let them speak to you before inserting them into a playlist.

- Cultivating a personal dancing mindfulness practice in a space at home, even if it's dancing around your living room, will not only help you grow as a facilitator, but it will also give you a forum to test out music and its emotional and visceral impact.

As with the element of breath, there are statements that I incorporate into classes that specifically invite awareness of the element of sound. Consider how some of these statements might work in a group you're facilitating or how they might deepen your personal practice.

- Bring your hand to your heart and just notice your own vibration for a moment. Think about your heartbeat as your own natural percussion.

- Know that you can check in with your heartbeat whenever you need to in the class; it will always tell you if you need more or less of something.

- When the tempo of our music changes, notice what's happening to your heartbeat.

- Are you remembering to check in with your heartbeat? Are you letting your heartbeat guide you?

- Check back in with your heartbeat. Notice what it's telling you.

As I advised with breath, feel free to set reminders around the space where you personally practice if you realize that awareness of sound is a struggle for you. The sticky-note reminder method also works with this element. However, I challenge you to consider how other aspects of your practice space at home can serve as reminders. Maybe there is a picture or a figurine in your space that corresponds to music or sound. For instance, on the shelf in my office, where I sometimes engage in dancing mindfulness practice, I have a doll playing a guitar that my grandmother gave me when I was younger. Whenever I see this doll, I am reminded to listen to the music and never take it for granted.

Weaving It All Together

My friend and colleague Dr. Paschal Baute is my personal role model for how to use music in this dance called life. As I mentioned earlier, Paschal is eighty-five years old and still dances with regularity. A former Roman Catholic priest who founded a successful interfaith ministry called the Spiritual Growth Network, he maintains an affiliation with the Celtic Christian Church and he continues to officiate at weddings. Paschal also served in some capacity (either in active duty or as a chaplain) in all four branches of the U.S. military. He whimsically shares in his talks that the Department of Veterans Affairs once declared him catastrophically disabled because of his physical limitations and partial blindness. Anyone who knows Paschal would agree that the term *catastrophically disabled* couldn't be further from the truth. Recently retired after a practice in clinical psychology spanning over forty years, Paschal continues to consult, write, and serve as a storyteller in his Kentucky community. His memoir is aptly titled *Resilience of a Dream Catcher*. Paschal embodies resilience, and he recently shared with me how dancing to music helps him thrive:

> I use dance regularly here at home, and so I heal my passionate heart of its many wounds ... with tears and laughter, joy and relief, peace and surrender, making my life a *yes* to all. I dance

to many kinds of music, Louis Armstrong, "Sunny Side of the Street," Beethoven, spiritual, "Prayer of St. Francis," Psalm 23, popular music of my generation, and favorite lyrics like "Send in the Clowns," depending upon my mood. I experience deep connectedness, release, freedom, wellness, resilience ... sometimes laughing and crying at the same time.

Even if I am no longer able to physically dance the way I'd like to at Paschal's age, I am hopeful that the music I love will allow me to dance mindfully. I am optimistic that the sounds of nature, like the clapping of the rivers or the wind singing through the mountains, as described in Psalms, will sustain my practice. I accept that as long as I have breath and a heartbeat, I have music within me. Living a life enriched by music and sound teaches me how to trust. I have faith in the process and can approach the rest of my life with a sense of nonstriving.

If we learn to trust the music of life and surrender to it, its various manifestations can unlock our curiosity and sense of adventure, give us the ability to release our rigid control over our body, and allow us to realize our capacity for rhythmic expression. It may take time and practice to form this kind of a relationship with music, yet allowing for that time and practice is a great way to cultivate the attitude of patience. Such a relationship is possible and it begins, in music's case, with trusting it. I hope that the practices shared in this chapter will help you to further develop this trust. Engaging in the practice that closes this chapter may allow you to further explore how this sense of trust connects to the other attitudes and to your life as a whole.

Try This: Sound, the Seven Attitudes, and the Creative Arts

The music of the universe attunes us to the process of living.

Are you listening?

What does listening teach you about the flow of life?

- Consider the seven foundational attitudes of mindfulness practice: nonjudging, patience, beginner's mind, trust, non-striving, acceptance, letting go.

- How does each attitude relate to sound? In response to this question, consider finding a song or a sound recording (nature sounds, ambient sounds) that corresponds to each attitude. Engage in a mindful listening experience with each selection and notice what happens within you—stillness? movement? a combination? What do you notice about your breath?

- How can the practice of fusing sound with movement help you to further develop these seven attitudes for your optimal health and well-being?

I encourage you to use dance, or any of the other creative arts, to contemplate these questions—get out your journal, your paints, your pencils, your camera—whatever helps you enter this place of contemplation. Perhaps you are a songwriter, a poet, or a fiction writer. Consider these channels to help you dance with the questions. Notice the connections that rise up when you fuse the practice of dancing mindfulness together with any of your other practices or creative pursuits.

Other Voices on Sound

Khan, Haznat Inayat. *The Music of Life* (Omega Uniform Edition of the Teachings of the Haznat Inayat Khan), 2nd ed. Keene, NH: Omega Publications, 1998.

Levitin, Daniel J. *This Is Your Brain on Music: The Science of a Human Obsession*. New York: Plume/Penguin, 2006.

Spotted Eagle, Douglas. *Voices of Native America: Instruments and Music*. Liberty, UT: Eagle's View Publishing, 1997.

Wade, Bonnie. *Thinking Musically: Experiencing Music, Expressing Culture*. New York: Oxford University Press, 2004.

Weisenberg, Joey. *Building Singing Communities: A Practical Guide to Unlocking the Power of Music in Jewish Prayer.* New York: Mechon Hadar, 2011.

Chapter 3

Body

A Vessel for Authenticity

The body is our general medium for having a world.
—*Maurice Merleau-Ponty,*
Phenomenology of Perception

Americans and citizens of other wealthy nations tend to equate body image with self-esteem. With the increasing impact of Westernization on global culture, this equation is now a factor in the developing world. When I lived in Bosnia and Croatia, it saddened me to see beautiful women starving themselves to look like Western supermodels. Although we tend to associate the issue of poor body image with women, men are affected by it as well. Individuals identifying as transgender or gender nonconforming often find themselves trying to sort out the set of rules and messages constructed in the gender binary (male and female) about how people *should* be in the world. This potentially adds to the wounds created by a society that cannot accept that gender is anything but male or female. Examples of these gender rules and messages are statements like these: "Boys and men aren't supposed to cry" and "Women must be a certain size to be desirable." Sometimes we receive these messages explicitly—a father may say something like "Big boys don't cry" when a young man shows emotion—or implicitly—absorbing years of advertising that shows only certain types of women being attractive to men. The pressure to look a certain way if you wish to realize all the promises of life is massive, for everyone, regardless of gender or sexual orientation. At least this is the message that the larger society would like us to believe.

The weight of this societal pressure (pun intended) crushed me for the majority of my life. As an awkward kid attending a gossipy Catholic school, I was always labeled the "fat kid" because I was one of the biggest girls in my class. Around the age of twelve, I dropped about forty pounds in order to seriously commit to figure skating, yet in skating circles I was still the fatso. Nonetheless, the talk at school was about how "good I looked" after dropping the weight. I received the message that shrinking in size made me a better person. The quick-fix dieting and weight loss industry makes billions of dollars each year, capitalizing on our fears and beliefs that we are somehow less of a person if we are overweight. I support maintaining a body weight that is healthy for the individual; Geneen Roth, author of *Women, Food, and God*, calls this the "natural weight." However, television shows such as *The Biggest Loser* disturb me, as do the bullying tactics employed on such shows.

Of all the chapters in the book, this one was the most emotionally charged for me to write because of my own struggles with body image and body hatred over the years. It wasn't until I discovered yoga and conscious dance practices that I grew into a greater acceptance of myself and my body. As a result, I became healthier. One of the reasons I created *Dancing Mindfulness* was to help other people grow into self-acceptance, to love and respect their bodies exactly as they are supposed to be. In this chapter, we will explore ways that healthy connection with and acceptance of your body can be achieved through dancing mindfulness practice.

The Body: Home to the Divine

Let's begin this exploration by consulting some time-honored teachings of the world's spiritual traditions for insight into the body. As communicated in the Anapanasati Sutra, the Buddha taught that contemplation of the body is one of the four foundations of mindfulness. The others are contemplation of feelings, the mind, and mental phenomena. The Buddha contended that breath meditation was the ideal practice for addressing all four in concert. Although breath is the foundation of mindfulness practice, including the practice of dancing mindfulness, there are many other practices for developing contemplation of the body. Even in traditional Buddhist circles, practices like walking meditation and other gentle movements are incorporated to provide stretching breaks for meditators. The great Buddhist teacher and monk Thich Nhat Hanh, author of a modern version of the Anapanasati Sutra,[1] published a lovely, user-friendly collection of such mindful movements, which he uses when leading retreats. Titled *Mindful Movements: Ten Exercises for Well-Being*, the book provides simple teachings on how to use moving meditation throughout the day (see "Other Voices on the Body," page 63).

The practice of yoga, originating in the pre-Vedic Indian tradition and later incorporated into certain practices of Hinduism, Buddhism, and Jainism, conveys a deep respect for the human body. Swami Vivekananda, a nineteenth-century Hindu monk venerated by many practitioners of modern yoga, proclaimed:

> The moment I have realized God sitting in the temple of every human body, the moment I stand in reverence before every human being and see God in him—that moment I am free from bondage, everything that binds vanishes, and I am free.[2]

Yoga is an eight-limbed path for physical, mental, and spiritual discipline and well-being, with two of the limbs, *pranayama* (breath) and *asana* (physical poses), directly working with the body. Although many Western views of yoga focus on these two limbs alone, the teachings of the entire path, in one way or another, help practitioners honor the completeness of their body. For instance, the ethical limbs of the yogic path (the *yamas* and the *niyamas*) teach principles such as *ahimsa* (nonharming), *mitahara* (measured diet), *saucha* (cleanliness), and *huta* (ritual and ceremony). Nicolai Bachman, a modern-day scholar on the Yoga Sutras, traditionally attributed to a sage named Pantañjali, explains that the entire yogic path gives us tools for living a kind, civil life. Additionally, the path gives us tools for "refining the body, mind, and sense organs; and turning our attention inward to understanding the true nature of the inner Self."[3]

A wisdom teaching from the Hindu tradition that resonates with many yogis and seekers along the spiritual path is that of the *koshas*, or sheaths. As described in the Taittiriya Upanishad, dated approximately sixth century BCE, there are five "bodies" comprising the human experience—the physical body (specifically the body that is nourished by food), the breath/energy body, the mind body (thinking), the intellect body (wisdom), and the bliss body (connection to our natural self). Noted therapist Susan Pease Banitt offers this explanation of the *koshas* for a modern-day audience:

> Imagine Russian nesting dolls sitting one inside of another. The *koshas* are like these dolls, only they interpenetrate and affect each other. They are the mechanisms that keep us separate from the divine in having our human experience.... Our *koshas*, wondrous though they are, keep us from experiencing our core [God, Brahman, the All That Is, Great Spirit, Allah], and thus we suffer. We "see through a glass darkly" thanks to the distracting and deluding power of the *koshas*. Not only that, but each sheath over time develops its own distortions, giving rise to illnesses and disease of all kinds. This process is natural, given that everything in the manifest universe is subject to entropy and decay. It is also a huge clue to our healing![4]

The *kosha* system offers a lovely lens through which we can behold the human body, insight that may seem strange if the only teachings we've received on the body have come from textbooks and modern media. Although the body in one sense is a physical vessel, it is much more than that; in dancing mindfulness practice we can view this ancient wisdom of the *koshas* by respecting our body as our total self, a vessel for authenticity. Visionary thought leader Jan Phillips weighs in on the impact of the faulty messages that many of us receive about the role of the body in our human journey:

> We are not here to transcend life, but to be fully immersed in it. Our bodies are not something we must triumph over. They are the medium of our transformation, the cauldron in which the elements of heaven and earth are steeped until they transmute one day into the being of which we are now the embryo. The journey we are on is a journey to fulfill this destiny, and we accomplish it through remembering our true nature, not through learning. We accomplish it by being true to our instincts, by listening to the wisdom of our bodies, and by abandoning with absolute fervor all notions of separateness and other.[5]

In my own multidenominational Christian background, I received many mixed messages about the body. When I see the passage from 1 Corinthians 3:16, proclaiming that my body is a temple of God's Holy Spirit, I can still recall fiery sermons from the pulpit interpreting this verse in a denigrating and abusive way. Underlying directives like Don't drink, Don't smoke, and Don't have sex outside of marriage was the notion that, if you do, you are defiling God's temple! The implied message I heard in all of that is if I defiled God's temple, then I didn't love God. Today I've arrived at a new understanding of this passage. I want to respect my body today not because some external force is shaming me, but because doing so honors the Divine in me. Moreover, I've learned that I am worthy of such respect. As Harvard professor Stephanie Paulsell so eloquently states:

> The Christian practice of honoring the body is born of the confidence that our bodies are made in the image of God's own goodness. As the place where the divine presence dwells, our bodies are worthy of care and blessing.... It is through our bodies that we participate in God's activity in the world.[6]

I did not come to my new understanding overnight; it took a great deal of self-compassionate spiritual practice, especially related to the mindfulness attitudes of acceptance and nonstriving. These practices, which include dancing mindfulness, allow me to honor my body as a vessel for transformation and authenticity.

A Vital Resource for Healing

As a trauma specialist, I believe that holistic treatment, which includes the body, is imperative for the treatment of trauma and stress-related disorders. The words of Kabbalah scholar and LGBTQI activist Dr. Jay Michaelson elegantly express one of my core beliefs:

> The body, independent of the heart's stirring and the misgivings of the intellect, is the site of holiness; even if there is no apparent change in the mind, and no softening of the heart, transformation takes place within the field of the body.[7]

Early in my counseling career, I discovered the transformative power of eye movement desensitization and reprocessing (EMDR) therapy. EMDR encourages individuals to notice sensations in the body as they reflect upon both positive and negative emotional stimuli. Bodily sensations are stimulated by bilateral eye movements, tactile "tapping" motions, or auditory stimulation through headphones.[8] Although EMDR incorporates body elements, it is still a kind of therapy that is used in an office without any significant movement. But when I began yoga and then conscious dance practice, all the bells and whistles began ringing in my head. First, I realized that dynamic, bilateral movement—that is, taking a walk, getting up and dancing, drumming, swimming—is an inherently powerful mechanism that we as human beings have to address stress and trauma stored at the body level. Second, the more aware I became of my own body responses, the more comfortable I became addressing body-level responses with patients and students.

There is a classic book in trauma studies called *The Body Never Lies*, by German psychologist Alice Miller. While I do not agree with everything she says in the book, the title of the book and much of the material in it continue to resonate with me strongly. Miller writes extensively about how unresolved traumatic responses manifest most significantly at the body level. So why isn't the body used more in the treatment of mental and emotional distress, at least in Western societies? As an example, traditional addiction treatment, a field in which I worked for many years, does a wonderful job of addressing the mental and spiritual components of addiction, but it overlooks the body. Through years of practice, I arrived at the clinical opinion that the reason addiction relapse rates are so high is that the body is not sufficiently incorporated into treatment. Other scholars who deal with trauma, namely Dr. Bessel van der Kolk, author of the aptly titled *The Body Keeps the Score: Brain, Mind, and Body in the Healing of Trauma*, and Dr. Gabor Mate, make similar contentions based on their analysis of research and practice.

I've distilled my studies in the areas of trauma, addiction, and mind-body medicine into this simple teaching: the body will signal what's going on within a person—emotionally, mentally, physically—ten steps before the rational mind will. Thus, learning to listen to the body's messages is a vital part of healing. A mindful dancing practice offers a powerful outlet for listening to the body's wisdom.

Setting Sail with Personal Practice

Cornelius Hubbard, a former student from my days coaching high school speech, played a significant role in my journey toward conceptualizing dancing mindfulness. Watching him move helped me realize the power in developing body awareness. I first met Cornelius when he was sixteen. I would have sworn that he clocked in many hours of formal dance training. Not only did he walk with grace, but he was also never afraid to break out into random intervals of dance while he was in the hallway waiting for his rehearsal time with me, or as a way to warm up at speech tournaments. He danced wherever he went, on a whim. Sometimes he danced like he was possessed— overcome with emotion, spirit, or simply the joy of the moment. He didn't take a formal dance class until he went to college, where he ended up minoring in dance. Whenever we spoke about his freedom in movement, the experience was never something he could quite verbalize. He simply said, "It's just in me." What if we could all remind ourselves of the need to tap into what is simply *in us* when we overly criticize our bodies and their limitations?

As Cornelius illustrated, your body is simply a vehicle through which you can access the world. Yet usually your body needs to be warmed up before you can go there! When I connected with Cornelius during his college studies, he introduced me to the concept of *noodling*—the art of moving your body randomly and fluidly like a piece of cooked spaghetti. It struck me that noodling could be used as a mindful movement to get into the vibe of dancing organically and mindfully. Sure, a world of emotion, spirit, and story may not come out of you right away, but the practice of noodling offers you a gateway to exploring organic movement.

Try This: Noodling

Haven't you ever envied a cooked noodle? The way it just slithers free and easy without any rigidity—this is an admirable quality that can teach us how to practice the attitude of letting go. For this practice, I challenge you to take on the role of a noodle and notice what happens.

- Come to your feet (as a modification, you can do this sitting or lying down). .

- With your next breath, think of taking on the role of a noodle. Begin by letting your shoulders roll around as if being jostled by bubbling-hot water, and then gradually loosen your body so that it easily rolls and sways, curls and furls like a cooked noodle.

- If it helps, think of yourself starting as an uncooked noodle or a long piece of pasta. Think of the space around you as hot water working on your stiffness, loosening your body into the form of a cooked noodle. Maybe al dente is all you can do at first—that's okay!

- Keep noodling in a mindful way for at least three minutes. Engage your beginner's mind, allowing your curiosity and sense of adventure to move your body in new and unfamiliar ways. If you try a movement that seems more rigid than fluid, don't be harsh on yourself or deem yourself a failure. Remember that nonjudgment and nonstriving—that is, enjoying the journey—are our goals here. The idea is to relax and explore new connections with your physical self.

- When you've completed the exercise, allow yourself to be still for a few moments longer (standing, sitting, or lying down). Notice how your body feels.

- Although you can do this in silence, it's lots of fun if you put on some music that can bring out your inner noodle! Explore—search your music collection and discover your favorite noodling song.

Dancing mindfulness is a fundamentally physical practice, so respecting your body as you begin working with it is important. There are other ways besides noodling to get into the groove of movement. In my facilitation of formal *Dancing Mindfulness* classes, I lead practitioners in a mindful, extended period of stretching as a way to honor the body and I certainly advise this for personal practice as well. It is not uncommon for my classes to include ten to fifteen minutes of stretch work and mindful movement to allow people to warm up their muscles and give them permission to connect with their bodies. Generally, I use a series of stretches that I have learned through my own yoga practice and I may vary them with each practice. If you are not familiar with yoga-style stretches or other gentle movements for warm-up, consult "Other Voices on the Body," page 63. Thich Nhat Hanh's *Mindful Movements* is one of my favorite resources to use as a starting point. You can also visit the online resource page connected to this book (www.dancingmindfulness.com/resources) for some of my favorite videos on yoga-based stretching. If you feel more comfortable starting your practice sitting in a chair instead of on the floor, you can also try the following practice, "Full Body Rising."

Try This: Full Body Rising

Standing up, for those of us with full leg function, is an action we do so mindlessly we take it for granted. However, it can feel really, really good if we pay attention to rising slowly and with purpose. Whenever we do an activity that is normally so automatic in a slow, mindful way, it is an ideal chance to cultivate the attitude of patience. Although this practice is written as if you were rising from a chair, you can modify it to rise from a sitting position on the floor.

- While in a sitting position, allow your upper body to fold over your seated, lower body. Your feet don't have to touch the ground; make the ground your aim and visual focus. Take a few moments and notice how it feels when the blood moves toward your head as you fold over.

- Very slowly and carefully, allow your buttocks to lift off the chair while remaining in the bent-over position. If your hands can touch your feet or the ground, do that; if not, just allow your hands to fall wherever they may on your legs.

- Hang out in this folded-over, "rag doll" position as long as you can.

- Slowly, mindfully begin to unfold your spine and rise. Think one vertebra at a time and avoid just rushing upright to standing.

- When you have totally unfolded, let your shoulders roll back and turn your gaze straight ahead, with confidence. Be present to the experience.

Modification

If you are unable to stand, you can still achieve the benefits of this exercise by doing the first part of bending over and then unfolding the spine. You can assume a confident posture in your upper body, even in a seated position.

Adding Music

Put on some music that creates a vibe of rising or emergence to enhance the mood of growing in confidence. The opening theme from *The Lion King* is one of my favorites for this purpose!

Resist the Urge to Compete

During warm-up stretch sequences, it is especially important to focus on the noncompetitive and nonstriving nature of dancing mindfulness. Rather than pushing hard to touch your toes, let your hands fall where they may, whether on your thighs, your knees, your calves, or maybe your ankles or feet. Pay attention to what your body is telling you and listen to its guidance. My first yoga teacher consistently proclaimed, "Touching your feet does not make you a better person." I've taken this wisdom to heart in my personal practice and I share it when facilitating others.

You can complete your stretching sequences on the ground, in a chair, or standing up. If you are starting on the ground or in a chair, use the process of coming up to your feet as another way to savor the experience of your practice. When I facilitate, I invite people to their feet in a slow and deliberate way so as to create an effect of growing like a flower or a tree. It can feel good to take your time coming to your feet, a process we so often rush!

How you order your beginning sequence of practice is completely up to you. Starting with noodling may feel more organic than stretching, or perhaps you'd like to stretch first and then noodle. Another important aspect of the beginning sequence is to explore the area in which you are dancing. There is such power in discovering our bodies in relation to the surrounding area. Here are some questions that might help you deepen your experience during this exploration period:

> What am I seeing in the space as I begin to move through it?
>
> Does something I see every day in my house or office appear new to me now that I'm dancing through the space?
>
> How does my body feel when I am aware of this newness?
>
> How do my feet move against this floor?

I had my own experience with the power of exploring space, as a practitioner, long after I developed *Dancing Mindfulness*. While teaching a trauma workshop at the Esalen Institute in California, I attended an afternoon class called "Dance Church," billed as a free-form improvisational class based on the work of conscious dance legends Gabrielle Roth and Vinn Marti. Dance church was unlike any conscious dance I ever experienced because the leader didn't utter a single word! The class was completely facilitated by his playlist and the collective, intentional vibe in the room. I walked in not knowing what to expect—the 4:30 p.m. class time began and so did the music. I thought he would get on the mic and provide some guidance. After about ten minutes, I realized this wasn't going to happen—people were just warming up and moving. So I used the time as an opportunity to practice dancing mindfulness. The music he played gave me a chance to come into my body on the floor, gradually get on my feet, and then explore the space. What I noticed the most was how my feet did not like the hardwood floor of the room—I'm used to dancing barefoot on hardwood laminate. In the spirit of curiosity and with the mind-set of a beginner I began moving my feet in new ways that felt better on the floor. In the process I found a whole new way of moving; a few new moves even came out of me that were especially healing. I relished learning how curiosity in mindful practice fosters the skill of adaptation, so vital in today's world. And from adaptation flows new creativity!

When you trust that dancing mindfulness is not a contest but rather a time and place of nonjudgmental support, you will be amazed by what your body can do. When I took my first conscious dance classes, movements I thought were long lost in my overweight body came back, like riding a bicycle. I continue to amaze myself as I practice dancing mindfulness. I shed inhibitions and realize there is beauty in modification. Sure, the moves don't look the same or come as easily as they did when I was thirteen, but the way I dance today feels wonderful in my late-thirties body. I generally have positive regard for my body and the process of mindful modification, but I'm not going to lie—sometimes I struggle to respect my body and its limitations. When this happens, I try to address those struggles in the context of mindful self-compassion that dancing mindfulness practice promotes. One day during the process of writing this book, I had a massive "I hate my body because it doesn't work the way I want it to" moment during a yoga class. I reached out to other *Dancing Mindfulness* facilitators in our online forum—my tribe of support—and disclosed what I was experiencing. The validation, the sharing of similar experiences, helped me to move through the issue with a greater sense of compassion. I realized that while body hatred may be normal, entertaining it certainly does not serve me. It doesn't serve you, either.

Working with Body Hatred, Grief, and Other Challenging Emotions

Personal practice is an ideal time to work through any hang-ups that you might have about your own body, its imperfections, and its limitations. There are several powerful ways you can address body image during personal practice. Beginning in either a sitting or a standing position, bring your hands to an area of your body with which you struggle the most—you may even hate that area. For me, the gut is my region of judgment. Cue up some music that is especially empowering to you, keep your hands on that area, and just go with the dance. A song like Kelly Clarkson's "Stronger" works really well for me in this practice, although you may connect with a different style of music for this work. Sometimes, I even like to use my stomach (which is ample) as a drum when I dance!

If your hatred of a particular body part or region is so immense, you may struggle with this exercise. If that's the case, just notice the struggle and honor it in a nonjudgmental way. Then ask your body what he or she most needs to either be with the struggle or dance through the struggle. It may be breathing techniques, prayer, a different kind of dance, or a tearful breakdown. Remember that journaling or other creative arts—painting, drawing, knitting, songwriting, playing music, taking pictures—can help you navigate this process and help you settle after the practice, if need be. If your emotional release is so deep that it does not seem to pass, consider seeking support from someone you trust, such as a therapist, a recovery sponsor, a good friend, a yoga teacher, a spiritual figure, or any other facilitator who can honor your struggle.

Although I have generally made peace with my body size, I still struggle with grieving the body I once had as a young, incredibly flexible teenage figure skater. I am still known to grunt in frustration when I visualize my body wanting to dance in a certain way but the mechanics do not cooperate. There are a couple of options that work well for personal practice in these cases. You can choose to sit with a certain piece of music and visualize yourself dancing in the way that you wish your body could dance. For some people, visualization is just as empowering as the movements themselves. After you've completed the visualization, move along to the next part of your practice and just dance with whatever emotions come up.

If grief emerges and it's something you feel comfortable moving with, you can dance with the experience of grief. You may consider asking yourself, "What am I grieving here?" It could be that you are grieving the body that you had at an earlier point in your life. Sometimes when I engage in this dance, I'm grieving the loss of dreams I had in my teenage years, such as figure-skating goals, relationships that didn't work out, not following through with some great career advice I got from a teacher because others made me believe it was too impractical. At times I can visualize myself back in those situations and I am moved to tears, yet either moving or sitting with those tears becomes a powerful vehicle for me to engage in the grief work that comes with letting go. I usually need to follow up with journaling or calling a trusted friend or support figure in recovery. Such personal practice dances are very powerful and ought not be entered into lightly. If your inner prompting is telling you that you are not yet ready for such a dance, honor that message.

Launching Out: Sharing the Practice with Others and Deepening Your Personal Practice

The urge to compete is heightened in a group setting, so it is especially important to focus on honoring the body. When I share the practice of dancing mindfulness, I encourage practitioners to pay attention to what their bodies are telling them. Through study with various yoga teachers and my own experiences developing *Dancing Mindfulness* classes, I've learned that teaching people to listen to the body's signals significantly reduces the risk of physical injury. Whenever it seems appropriate in a class, I use the following facilitation statements to foster awareness of the body:

- Stretching ought to feel good. Never stretch to the point of pain.

- Think about a stretch as a gradual warming of your muscles. If they start to feel like they're on fire, back off.

- You may notice in this class that others are moving in a vigorous way. Some people may look like trained dancers. Please know there is *never* an obligation to keep up.

- Honor where you are, today.

- If at any time your body is telling you that you need a drink of water or you need to sit out a dance, honor that prompt and take care of yourself.

- What is your body telling you, right now?

- Are you remembering to listen to your body?

As part of guiding people to get in touch with their bodies, I include familiarization of the dance space as part of the warm-up. First I invite people to just work with their feet against the floor—or the earth, if we're outside—while staying in a hula-hoop–size area. Then I encourage them, if they are feeling moved, to take their movement out into the space of the room. Some facilitation statements I make during this process related to the body include the following:

- Notice the connection between your feet and your knees. Then notice the connection between your knees and your hips.

- Be aware of your shoulders, an area where we hold so much stress. How does it feel to move them through our space, to music?

- Let your feet carry you where your heart and spirit are telling you to go.

If you need more guidance for these opening sequences, visit the Dancing Mindfulness resource page (www.dancingmindfulness.com/resources).

After the warm-up, you can take your *Dancing Mindfulness* group in myriad directions, finding opportunities to nurture self-acceptance through mindful movement. Consider incorporating into your classes whatever songs speak to you in your personal practice. One of my favorite dances to lead, something I usually do after an emotionally charged middle portion of class, is what I like to call a "Runway Dance." Although I'm sure this dance is not radically original, I was inspired to create my version of it while contemplating society's pressure on each of us to look like a super-model in order to be loved. This pressure crushes so many people, especially women.

Try This: Runway Dance

- Invite participants to form two parallel lines facing each other, creating ample space in between for a "runway."

- Anyone who wants to can take a turn "working it" down the runway, showing their "inner supermodel to the world." This is the spirit of the dance and how I introduce it. Feel free to adapt this concept to your own language and style.

- As the facilitator, I generally go first as a way of modeling, and then I invite people to come down one at a time as it is their turn in the line. Of course, taking your turn on the catwalk is optional; there's no pressure to participate.

- Encourage everyone else in the lines to clap, shout encouragement, or otherwise support those who are strutting their stuff.

- Make sure that everyone who wants to has a chance to take a turn. In large groups, this may mean that you have to add a song to accommodate. If people are too shy to go down the runway by themselves, you can also encourage them to strut their stuff two at a time. Sometimes after everyone has taken a turn and there is some music left over, I suggest that participants go down the runway in pairs.

- In my experience, both supporting others and receiving support can be empowering.

From Jamie's Music Box:
Empowering Your Runway Dance

When you are facilitating for a large class or at a conference, the energy in a Runway Dance can be amazing. Songs like the following work nicely for the Runway Dance:

- "Vogue" or "Express Yourself" (Madonna)

- "Born This Way" (Lady Gaga)

- "I'm Too Sexy" (Right Said Fred)

- "Supermodel" (RuPaul)

- "I Am What I Am" (Gloria Gaynor)

Just as warming up your body is an important way to honor it, so too is cooling down your body, in both group and personal practice. I discuss this idea further in chapter 7 on fusion. Before inviting people into a period of relaxation (*sivasana*) and integration, I choose a piece of music with a slower tempo.

If you decide to end your practice on the floor or in a chair, I encourage you to do some variation of a twist. Either a simple seated twist on both the right and left side or a lying-down, supine twist is an excellent way to bring the body back to equilibrium after a vigorous dance practice. You can visit the yoga links on the resource website for this book if you need more visual guidance about twisting. For the final songs on any given playlist, I issue some variation of the following invitation:

> Listen to your body. Ask your body what it most needs right now before preparing for relaxation. Maybe there's one more dance to be danced on your feet. Maybe there are some standing poses that would feel really good to your body right now.

Or maybe your body is telling you that it's time to return to the earth. Whatever your body is telling you, honor it.

In my personal practice, I use this same cool-down invitation, asking myself, "What does my body need the most in this moment before coming back to the earth for final meditation/relaxation?" If you primarily engage in dancing mindfulness practice outside of a group, it might even be a nice idea to make a simple recording on your phone or other device to play back—in your voice—toward the end of your practice. You can use the script that I present here, or come up with your own unique invitation into integration and hopefully relaxation.

As part of closing, I invite participants to thank their bodies for showing up to practice dancing mindfulness, for taking a risk in trying something new. With gratitude you honor your body for being what it is.[9] Expressing this gratitude is also a regular part of my personal practice. Whether during the cool-down or at some other point in your personal practice, I hope you will find an opportunity to express gratitude for the gift of your body.

Try This: Sit Down and Dance Mindfully

I've had the great privilege of facilitating many *Dancing Mindfulness* classes where participants need to sit down and either observe or do what they can from a seated position. So many variations are possible because *Dancing Mindfulness* is a practice that honors variation. Here are some guidelines and best practices drawn from my experience:

- Inform participants that sitting alongside the perimeter of the space, either on a cushion or in a chair, is always an option. I establish the perimeter guideline for the safety of other participants.

- Let participants know that they are invited to move in whatever way they can, or however they wish to modify, from a chair. In my experience, I've witnessed both the injured and the elderly engage their upper bodies, even though their lower bodies need to take it easy.

- The only guideline I issue to those who observe is to be respectful of those who are practicing in the space. It is important for all who are involved to honor the space and the practice as sacred. Many people who have opted out of a class due to disability or for other reasons have shared with me that observing a *Dancing Mindfulness* class can be a powerful experience in and of itself.

- The facilitator and other dancers may reach out to those who are observing, either with a smile or with an inclusive gesture. For instance, I like to come up to people who are observing, if their demeanor seems open, and bow *namaste*. However, never force a person to dance or invite her to get up. If observers want to get up or otherwise respond to your approach, they will. Let them take the lead.

- If a person with a disability that proves to be an injury risk for him or for others wants to take the class, ask him if you can assign someone to dance with him as a guide, purely for safety reasons. A blind gentleman came to my class at a retreat; he really wanted to move, but he understood the safety risk and allowed one of my regular students to be his personal guide through the class. Evaluate these situations on a case-by-case basis.

Weaving It All Together

There are a variety of implications for how dancing mindfulness practice—either as a personal practice or as a group practice—can be used to honor and heal the body. Having the privilege of sharing the practice with clinical clients, students in the community, and professional colleagues, I steadily receive new feedback about how dancing mindfulness makes an impact. People share the positive effect of dancing mindfulness practice on healing from addictions, trauma, and physical illness. Dancing mindfulness can be a companion through times of transition, like job loss or the death of a loved one, and it can serve as an artistically dynamic coping mechanism when you feel stuck in some stressful life situation, like graduate school, a stagnant long-term relationship, or chronic illness.

Professional counselor and cancer survivor Natalie Fryar shares how a group *Dancing Mindfulness* experience at a conference helped her to release some of the trauma still playing out in her body. She reflects:

> My first experience with dancing mindfulness was at a professional conference I attended in Atlanta, Georgia. This conference was my initiation back to work. I was diagnosed with breast cancer earlier in the year and had gone through a double mastectomy as well as chemo. On day three of the conference I waddled onto the atrium grounds ready to hear about this *Dancing Mindfulness* thing and what I got was an initiation into my own personal healing. Since being diagnosed with cancer I had not moved—physically. I felt frozen in my body with fear because of what cancer and chemo had done to me. Through my participation in this "training to help others," I found a release that I could not explain. It was exhilarating to be able to be free to move my body in a way that I hadn't in months. It not only gave me a personal healing experience that I will continue to pursue, but it also helped me professionally to bridge the gap in therapy for my clients.

What can your body teach you about yourself? Perhaps you've explored this question in other spiritual practices, or maybe it's a question that hasn't even crossed your mind. Whether you've been dancing with the question for many years or whether you are new to body-intensive work, I hope that the practices presented in this chapter offer you some guidance in your process of discovery. Some of you may struggle with the "body is a temple" idea offered in Corinthians and implied in other sacred traditions. If that is the case, as you set out on this discovery, consider this modification from one of my favorite tell-it-like-it-is voices, chef Anthony Bourdain: "Your body is not a temple, it's an amusement park. Enjoy the ride."[10]

Try This: Body, the Seven Attitudes, and the Creative Arts

Your body is your vehicle for the dance of your life.

What can your body teach you about yourself?

What can your dancing body teach you about authenticity and self-compassion?

• Consider the seven foundational attitudes of mindfulness practice: nonjudging, patience, beginner's mind, trust, non-striving, acceptance, letting go.

• How does each attitude relate to the body? Consider putting a physical movement or gesture to each attitude and be curious about what you notice in your body when you come into that movement.

• How can the body in motion help you to further develop these seven attitudes for your optimal health and well-being?

I encourage you to use dance, or any of the other creative arts, to contemplate these questions—get out your journal, your paints, your pencils, your camera—whatever helps you enter this place of contemplation. Perhaps you are a songwriter, a poet, or a fiction writer. Consider these channels to help you dance with the questions. Notice the connections that rise up when you fuse the practice of dancing mindfulness together with any of your other practices or creative pursuits.

Other Voices on the Body

Bachman, Nicolai. *The Path of the Yoga Sutras: A Practical Guide to the Core of Yoga*. Boulder, CO: SoundsTrue, 2011.

Banitt, Susan Pease. *The Trauma Toolkit: Healing PTSD from the Inside Out*. Wheaton, IL: Quest Books, 2012.

Hanh, Thich Nhat. *Mindful Movements: Ten Exercises for Well-Being*. Berkeley, CA: Parallax Press, 2008.

Miller, Alice, and Andrew Jenkins. *The Body Never Lies: The Lingering Effect of Hurtful Parenting*. New York: W.W. Norton & Co, 2006.

Parnell, Laurel. *Tapping In: A Step-by-Step Guide to Activating Your Healing Resources Through Bilateral Stimulation*. Boulder, CO: SoundsTrue, 2008.

Roth, Geneen. *Women, Food, and God: An Unexpected Path to Almost Everything*. New York: Scribner, 2011.

Shapiro, Francine, and Margot Silk Forrest. *EMDR: The Breakthrough "Eye Movement" Therapy for Overcoming Stress, Anxiety, and Trauma*. New York: Basic Books, 1997.

Chapter 4

Mind

Bringing Us Home to the Present Moment

This one a long time have I watched. All his life has he looked away ... to the future, to the horizon. Never his mind on where he was. Hmm? What he was doing.

—*Master Yoda,* The Empire Strikes Back

Mandy is one of my dearest friends, teachers, and collaborators. A successful yoga instructor and budding *Dancing Mindfulness* facilitator, she is the embodiment of a survivor. A recovering drug addict struggling with post-traumatic stress disorder since childhood, Mandy's story is something you might see in a movie about hitting bottom and then bouncing back with glorious redemption. She now uses her experience and her commitment to the yogic lifestyle in working with others on healing from distress. Mandy publically attests to the transformative impact of yoga and conscious practices in her life. It's a great honor to offer collaborative workshops with her on overcoming trauma through yoga. I experience such bliss when I am a student in one of her classes, sinking into a restorative position like *legs up the wall* and hearing her intone a modern interpretation of Lao Tzu:

> When you are depressed, you are living in the past. When you are anxious, you are living in the future. Just allow yourself to be in the present.

I've heard countless variations on that statement from professors, therapists, self-help figures, and yoga instructors. Yet I experienced such an epiphany the first time I took a yoga class with Mandy and heard her express it just this way. Mindful practice is about allowing the mind to steady and simply be in the *now*. By consistently engaging in the practice of coming back to the here and now, we can allow the chains binding us to the past to fall away. Through mindful practice we can remain grounded and unaffected by the suction of the future, pulling us toward worry about things we cannot control.

The mind is not our enemy. By engaging in consistent practice we can learn to understand the intricacies of how our mind operates in our individual experiences. This consistent practice teaches us how to let our mind work for us, not against us. As a result, we can always come home to the present moment. Too often we see the mind only as an instrument for thinking—an instrument that can run amok with worry and negative ruminating if left unchecked. However, our mind is so much more than our thoughts. Consider that both the breath and the body—elements of dancing mindfulness that we've already covered—are guided by mental processes. As we will explore in this chapter, we have a "thinking" or more rational mind, an emotional mind, and a mind that regulates physicality. Some spiritual traditions offer the concepts of a wisdom mind and a spirit or bliss mind, the mental conduit that allows us to connect with spirit. While we can dance with the element of mind in a variety of ways in dancing mindfulness practice, I typically regard the mind as the vehicle that allows for integration of our human experience. As in Native American spirituality, the body, the mind, and the spirit cannot be separated.

The Mind as More Than the "Brain"

To further explore the concept of the mind as a vehicle for integration, a core teaching of dancing mindfulness, let's place this in the context of philosophy, sacred tradition, and basic biology. In Buddhist meditation circles, teachers often ask us to contemplate what makes the brain different from the mind. The question is a wonderful contemplative exercise because it is so open to debate and discussion. Fully explaining these debates on the brain, the mind, and consciousness extends beyond the scope of this book, but Christina Sarich, yoga journalist and founder of Yoga for the New World, offers a solid overview:

> The mind vs. brain debate has been going on since before Aristotle. He and Plato argued that the soul housed intelligence or wisdom and that it could not be placed within the physical body. In a well-described version of dualism, Descartes identifies mind with the consciousness and self-awareness of itself, with an ability to distinguish itself from the brain, but still called the brain the seat of intelligence. In yogic science, the mind is considered to be pure vibrating energy. It is an element (non-physical by nature) which conducts "thought" faster than the speed of light and retains all experience whether consciously addressed by the thinker or not. It can create substance from nothing. It contains the aura, or energy body, and can project to other minds, and receive from them also. It communicates in the language of feeling. It has a profound effect on the energy level of the physical body, which temporarily houses it, and has the capacity to heal its own physical house as well as that of others. It is often referred to as a Spark of the Divine or as a wave on the vast limitless ocean of the cosmic ever-present possibility of what is. Our minds, due to their nature as a spark or wave of a much greater, infinite intelligence, are capable of unbelievable things.[1]

In my own pondering of the differences between brain and mind, I arrived at this general conclusion: the brain is the biological instrument that houses the mind and allows for its function.

Spiritual teachings in various traditions offer perspectives on the marvel that is the human mind. In chapter 3, we briefly reviewed the *kosha* system originating in Hindu teachings. This system presents rational thinking and wisdom as distinct, and distortions in this system can keep us from union with our core (that is, total union with the Divine). Also notice that within the *kosha* system, the functions of thinking and wisdom, typically viewed by Western science as mental processes, are considered bodies. According to the Anapanasati Sutra,[2] the Buddha taught that contemplating the body, feelings, mind, and mental phenomena are all important in the practice of mindfulness meditation. Mental phenomena include mental states, the arising of and departing of each state, and examination of the factors that include each arising and departing. Putting body, feelings, mind, and mental phenomena together suggests that they are inextricably linked.

Another teaching that attests to this union can be found in the desert monasticism of early Christianity. Pseudo-Marcarius, a fourth-century Syrian monk, reflected:

> For the heart directs and governs all other organs of the body. And when grace pastures the heart, it rules over all the members and the thoughts. For there, in the heart, the mind abides as well as the thoughts of the soul and all its hopes.[3]

In speaking about the connection between heart and mind, Pseudo-Marcarius recognized a reality that we've come to embrace in the study of modern neuroscience. What he poetically calls the organ of the heart is a reference to the emotional mind, which really does exist at the center of the human brain.

Three as One: The Triune Brain

The brain allows for the mind to unfurl its marvelous possibilities and connections to the other elements we access in dancing mindfulness practice. The human brain is one of the most complex systems in the universe. When we refer to the "human brain," we are actually talking about three distinct brains that are working together as one whole. If you are familiar with the Christian theology of the Trinity, the human brain can be described in similar terms: three persons as one God, like three brains operating as one brain. To take this metaphor a step further, even the most seasoned theologians in the Christian tradition can find themselves flummoxed at the prospect of trying to explain the Trinity. And so it goes with the brain.[4]

In my own study, I've found the three-brain, or triune-brain, teaching to be the most helpful concept in understanding that my mind is more than just my thoughts. The three brains comprising the human brain can be colloquially described as the "lizard" brain, the emotional brain, and the rational brain. Each brain developed during separate times in our evolutionary history, and each operates with its own respective senses of time, space, and memory.[5]

- **The "Lizard Brain"** (properly called the reptilian brain or the brainstem). Often referred to as the "lizard brain," the brainstem controls the functions that you, as a human being, have in common with a lizard. This oldest and lowest part of the brain is located at the base of your brain, moving into the brainstem. The lizard brain controls reflex behaviors, muscle control, balance, breathing, and heartbeat; it reacts to direct stimulation. This is the brain that allows for physical movement and it is where our flight-fight-freeze reaction originates.

- **The "Emotional Brain"** (properly called the limbic brain or the midbrain, as it dwells in the center of a human brain). This brain is the source of emotions and instincts, including attachment, survival, and learning. When this part of the brain is triggered, emotion is activated. Hence, when we have life experiences that are emotionally charged, the lessons we learn about ourselves, whether they are positive or negative, have a greater tendency to stick. This part of the brain contains the systems that regulate pain and pleasure responses. Our flight-fight-freeze responses, originating in the lizard brain, may appear different, from one person to another, based on our emotional learning patterns. For instance, a lot of attention has been given to the "tend and befriend" (that is, the caregiving) response in women as an instinctual mechanism for coping with stress. People who use drugs, alcohol, food, or other rewarding behaviors are essentially doing it to relieve distress in this brain. This brain is also called the mammalian brain because all mammals have one. If you have a dog, cat, or other pet, and you've been able to form an empathetic relationship with that animal, the functions that allow for the formation of such relationships are housed in this brain. Although the expressions of empathy, love, and compassion are more finely tuned in the rational brain, the raw experience of the emotions that fuel them originate here.

- **The "Rational Brain"** (properly called the neocortex or the cerebral cortex). This brain is unique to primates. This brain regulates our higher-order thinking skills—reason, speech, meaning, and self-awareness—as well as the function of sapience (the wisdom to know the difference). This brain is sometimes referred to as the "new brain" or the "highest brain" because it is what distinguishes us as primates from the rest of the animal kingdom. The rational brain is also responsible for time, chronology, and organization; it's the brain that lets you know that you are in the here and now, while the past happened at some point in the past. This is the brain that is prone to getting shut down when our emotions overtake us. On the other side of that coin, relying too heavily on these rational functions of our brain, like critical thinking, analysis, and talking, can keep us cut off from what our emotions and our body have to teach us.

We rely on all three brains to function harmoniously. When we are emotionally wounded, the communication between the three parts can break down, causing us to get trapped, for example, in survival mode, unable to access our rational wisdom. There are many ways in which this sense of discord between the three brains can manifest in the human experience. We might find ourselves able to talk about things that happened to us in our past, we might be full of spiritual awareness or insight into our lives, but we may still be cut off from our emotions and our body. We might find ourselves behaving irrationally when a life stressor causes discomfort in our physical body because that discomfort is reminiscent of something that happened in the past. Although our rational mind tells us that the past is in the past and that we are safe in the here and now, the other brains may have something else to say. Listening to these messages, instead of avoiding or suppressing them, is a potentially challenging yet ultimately powerful way to come home to the present moment. If we do not hold space for them, they will keep surfacing in some way until we can practice nonjudgmental, acceptance-filled hospitality for what they are trying to teach us.

As a therapist and trauma survivor myself, I fully recognize that coming back to the here and now is easier said than done. (Hint, hint: Why do you think mindfulness is called a *practice*?) Moreover, an unresolved traumatic experience or series of experiences can imprint powerfully negative messages onto our emotional brain. These negative beliefs, if left unaddressed, can become the filters through which we see the world. So if a traumatic or highly stressful experience taught you "I am defective," that belief will stay with you if you are not afforded the opportunity to work through it in a safe and supportive way. When negative beliefs about the self are deeply ingrained, they become part of you. You might find it virtually impossible to shift to positive thinking without a major spiritual experience or some form of visceral-level catharsis. It takes more than just thinking or talking to dislodge this negative obstacle; healing occurs through action and connection.

A variety of therapeutic approaches, such as eye movement and desensitization reprocessing (EMDR) therapy, body-centered psychotherapy, focusing, dialectical behavior therapy (DBT), and many others, are aimed at helping people overcome these negative traps in a holistic way. Plenty of self-help approaches prove helpful to many, such as *The Work* by Byron Katie. Twelve-step and other support groups can also help people navigate these vital shifts, especially when a person is working the steps and connecting with other recovering individuals in a meaningful way. Dancing mindfulness practice is one more way to address these negative beliefs.

Setting Sail with Personal Practice

Mindfulness practice is the process of teaching our mind to work for us, not against us. I get sad when I hear people say things like this: "I can't meditate. There's no way I can turn my mind off." Unfortunately, this stereotype about meditation has taken hold because of popular portrayals of meditation practice as an instantaneously quiet experience. Mindfulness practice is not about turning the mind off. If anything, it's about turning it on—developing a greater sense of awareness of your experiences and what they can teach you about yourself. Consistent engagement in mindfulness practices that involve activity—exercise, breathwork, journaling, drawing, prayer, dreaming, and, of course, dancing—can help us break through the survival blockage to help us address our emotional wounds. In essence, they allow us to tune and then fine-tune the instrument of our mind. In dancing mindfulness, for example, we remind ourselves to come back to awareness, to honor the present, and to consider the possibilities of creativity and healing.

Try This: What Does the *Mind* Mean to Me?

On any given day, I can log onto Facebook or Twitter and ask my friends, "What does the mind mean to you?" and I get a flurry of responses. No two responses are the same. Some friends answer with exquisite poetry about how they've come to befriend their minds. Others provide negatively charged responses in the vein of "My mind is a dangerous place to be for too long" or "My mind is something that I lose all the time." Occasionally, I will get a pop-culture-slogan response like this: "The mind is a terrible thing to waste." As we've discussed in this chapter, there are many different ways to describe, to define, and to conceptualize the mind. Your definition of the mind is what's most important in this moment as you cultivate your personal dancing mindfulness practice. Let's engage in an exercise designed to help you explore your relationship with your mind.

- Take a moment to come into stillness. Take several deep breaths, if needed, to help you come into this stillness. You may start this exercise sitting, standing, or lying down.

- After spending a few moments arriving at this stillness with the help of your breath, bring up the question, "What does the mind mean to me?"

- You may not come up with a response right away—that's okay, if that's the case. Just continue to breathe with a sense of nonstriving (that is, not forcing the issue).

- When you notice your immediate response, be still and stay with it in a spirit of nonjudgment for the next several moments. It may shift; it may not.

- After this period of stillness, begin to invite some movement into your body. Put on some music, preferably without lyrics. This exercise can be done in silence as well. It may be interesting to begin your movement in silence and then bring in some music, noticing if the music changes anything.

- See what develops as you continue to dance with this question of "What does the mind mean to me?" Different insights, thoughts, and emotions may surface as you just keep moving.

Maybe something that is coming up is calling you to a mix of stillness and movement.

- Listen to your inner wisdom regarding when to stop—one song might be sufficient, or you may want to keep going with this process.

- When you transition from this practice, consider coming back into a seated stillness and notice that experience, or you may journal to reflect on what came up for you as you danced with this important question. How might your insights help you in your dancing mindfulness practice and in your life as a whole?

Greeting Your Guests

Personal dancing mindfulness practice can be taken in many directions because so many human experiences are made possible by the mind. You may work most effectively with the element of mind during the portions of your practice where you choose to come into a more traditional seated meditation. Some people practice dancing mindfulness best by alternating between several minutes of silent, seated practice and several minutes of moving to music. This shift gives you a beautiful opportunity to notice the interplay between stillness and movement. Ask yourself: What does the stillness teach me about my movement, and what does the movement teach me about my stillness? Perhaps a recurring thought, like the prospect of finishing a mile-long to-do list, keeps creeping in. Do I need to sit with that thought or move with it? Perhaps heavy emotions will arise, like sadness or anger. A core negative belief about yourself, such as "I can't succeed" or "I am damaged," may cry out for attention. In my experience, both stillness and movement may be required to greet those thoughts, emotions, and beliefs in a nonjudgmental way. Greeting them nonjudgmentally and being open to the flow of such awareness can help us build acceptance, patience, and trust—both in the practice and in ourselves.

Mindfulness teachers in the modern era often recite "The Guest-house," a classic poem by thirteenth-century Sufi mystic Rumi. In this poem, Rumi calls us to treat our minds as a guesthouse for whatever may come. Joy, sorrow, dark thoughts, shame, and malice must all be treated as guides from beyond. Consider seeking out a full version of the poem to inspire your dancing mindfulness practice.[6] What I always liked about the metaphor of the guesthouse is that I can enter-tain whatever may come but, as with guests passing through, a sense of impermanence is implied. This impermanence helps me embrace a phrase like *This too shall pass*. I recognize that I don't have to be con-sumed by whatever my thoughts, emotions, or beliefs are teaching me during any given practice or season of life.

In my experience, any dancing mindfulness practice enables heal-ing as you let go. You can dance to help you let go of a stressor or a nagging thought that is plaguing you or you can dance to let go of something that might have more of an emotional charge. Allow me to share a very personal story of loss. In my view, loss is a wound—a trauma—that needs healing attention, like any other wound. Losses that shake us to the core of our being need extra care and attention. This loss happened when I had been sober almost a decade, I had many years of experience as a trauma counselor, and I had spent a great deal of time practicing yoga. Shortly after my first marriage ended, I reconnected with an old high school boyfriend, a dear figure from my past whom I long regarded as the one who got away. We had a passionate, fiery love affair for the better part of a year, and everything in me believed that some cosmic force was bringing us back into each other's lives. The way I was able to open up my heart to him again surprised me. So when he made it very clear that he could not commit to giving me what I wanted because he never saw himself getting married or having children, I was crushed. It was the ultimate case of two people who loved each other deeply, but could not be together because of who we were as people. The grief when this relationship crumbled was unlike any I had ever experienced— worse than any death; even worse than my divorce. At one point I fell into a very deep depression that seriously interfered with my ability to function in my work life.

Looking back, I recognize that mindfulness practices helped me ride out this loss and adapt to it, so it didn't destroy me. Moving mindfulness meditations, like yoga and dance, and simple practices like breathwork, proved critical to my survival and recovery. When the feelings came, I surfed the waves of emotion, breathing through my tears and making a commitment not to judge myself at any juncture for feeling what I was feeling. The dancing mindfulness I practiced, even prior to formally developing the *Dancing Mindfulness* class structure, helped me transform my grief into beauty. I practiced letting go of that great love, and, as a result, the path cleared and my heart was open for my current husband to come into my life. We share a passionate love and a complementary vision of life, a manifestation of the trust I developed in practicing mindfulness. As much as I believe in formal psychotherapy, I don't think that anything could have helped me grieve the loss of the one relationship and prepare my heart for the other as effectively as mindfulness practice did, especially the practice of dancing mindfulness.

Not all healing experiences are of this magnitude, but that doesn't mean the smaller episodes of healing can't have a significant impact on your life. Even if you engage in dancing mindfulness primarily for fun and accessing the joy of movement, you can move with the intention of "letting go of" or "shaking off" negativity. Think about the noodling practice presented in chapter 3. Put it together with a song that encourages you to "shake" and notice what happens with your movement, your thoughts, and your emotions. Tunes like Florence + the Machine's "Shake It Out," Taylor Swift's megahit "Shake It Off," KC and the Sunshine Band's "Shake, Shake, Shake," or even old MGM classics like "Shakin' the Blues Away" are ideal. You can also take this practice of shaking it off to deeply spiritual places (covered in chapter 5).

Dancing with Demons and Delights

Dancing mindfully with the element of the mind allows us to do some deep work on both our positive and negative beliefs about ourselves.

If you are new to the practice of using dance in such a way, I suggest that you begin with the practice of dancing with positive beliefs or affirmations before moving on to work with the negatives.

Try This: Dancing with Our Positive Beliefs
(with Jamie's Music Box Recommendations)

In this practice, I invite you to choose a positive belief about yourself that you hold to be true. It's okay if it doesn't seem completely true every day.

- Scan this list of popular positive affirmations and notice what pops out at first glance:

> I am good enough.
> I am a good person.
> I am whole.
> I am blessed.
> I am unique.
> I am worthy.
> I am significant.
> I am important.
> I deserve to live.
> I deserve only good things.
> I am smart.
> I can belong.
> I am special.
> I am a success.
> I am beautiful.
> My body is sacred.
> I did/do my best.
> I do the best I can with what I have.
> I can be trusted.
> I can make friends.
> It's okay to make mistakes.

I can only please myself.
I cannot please everyone.
I can trust myself.
I can choose whom to trust.
I am safe now.
I can create my sense of safety.
I can show my emotions.
I am in control.
I have power now.
I can help myself.
I have a way out.
I have options.
I can get what I want.
I can succeed.
I can stand up for myself.
I can let it out.

- Trust that whatever affirmation caught your attention first is the best starting place. Perhaps you are in a place where you struggle to accept this positive affirmation as true in the moment.

- Consider using that affirmation as a goal statement, as something you are moving toward in your life. Sometimes I call this the "Fake it 'til you make it" dance, if seeing this practice as a dance to manifest positive intention doesn't quite work for you.

- Choose a song, perhaps a song from your collection that corresponds to your desired affirmation. Dance with it, being present to whatever experiences may arise. If your goal is "I can stand up for myself," a song like Sara Bareilles's "Brave" or the classic Queen power anthem "We Will Rock You" might help you reach the intended vibration. Cue up the music and dance as if you are someone who already believes she can stand up for herself and just notice what happens.

- You may connect with the desired intention in a new and meaningful way. You may then consider moving your next dance into an area that pictures you going out into the world and putting this goal into action. How does a person who can stand up for herself dance? What movements do you associate with a person who is assertive and empowered?

Dancing with this positive belief and matching music may not feel genuine because you are not yet ready. You may find it difficult to move. Just noticing that experience will likely reveal the negative belief or issue that you *will* have to move through to experience healing. Dancing through your proverbial mental demons is powerful practice. I invite you to begin by visualizing your goals and dreams for yourself. Think of where you want to be, and then notice what negative beliefs are keeping you from realizing that goal.

Taking your personal practice to this level must be handled with caution. If you do not feel that you are ready to dance in this way, honor that inner knowing. As with any potentially cathartic work, you must prepare for it and have reasonable assurance that you can handle what may or may not surface. If you already engage in personal practice with the breath, body, and spirit elements, you will likely be in a better position to dance with the following practice. Because all the elements of dancing mindfulness practice are interrelated, your work in one element can support you in another. If your emotional release in this personal practice makes you feel unsafe, seek support from someone you trust, like a therapist, a recovery sponsor, a good friend, a yoga teacher, a spiritual presence in your life, or any other facilitator who can ease your mind.

This is a list of some common negative beliefs that weigh people down emotionally, physically, and spiritually. Scan through the list. As with the positive affirmations list, notice what jumps out at you first. If you feel confident enough to self-direct your dancing mindfulness practice at this point, start working to change that belief in whatever way feels organic.

- I am not good enough.
- I am a bad person.
- I am permanently damaged.
- I am defective.
- I am terrible.
- I am worthless/inadequate.
- I am insignificant.
- I am not important.
- I deserve to die.
- I deserve only bad things.
- I am stupid.
- I do not belong.
- I am different.
- I am a failure.
- I am ugly.
- My body is ugly.
- I am alone.
- I should have known better.
- I should have done something.
- I did something wrong.
- I am to blame.
- I cannot be trusted.
- I cannot trust myself.
- I cannot trust anyone.
- I am in danger.
- I am not safe.
- I cannot show my emotions.
- I am not in control.
- I have to be perfect.
- I have to please everyone.
- I am weak.
- I am trapped.
- I have no options.
- I cannot get what I want.

- I cannot succeed.
- I cannot stand up for myself.
- I cannot let it out.
- I am powerless/helpless.

This list is not exhaustive. Glancing over it may elicit other ideas about what is keeping you stuck. You may notice that one or two beliefs jump out at you, or it may seem as if the whole list applies to you. If it seems as if many of these beliefs apply, go back over the list and see which ones register the greatest response in your body. By way of example, maybe you notice your muscles starting to tighten or you begin to sweat. A chill may come over you, or you may notice tingling sensations when you see that negative belief in print. Those are likely the beliefs that you will need to take to your dance practice.

Try This: Dancing with Our Negative Beliefs

- Bring to mind a goal that you have—a dream you cherish, the destiny you desire. Give yourself some time to fully visualize that destiny.

- Looking deeply within yourself and, staying with your movement, think about what is keeping you from realizing your vision. What's the block? What is the nasty belief you hold about yourself that keeps you from moving in the direction of your dreams? Don't overthink it; just notice what comes up. Start moving with that belief. If it seems organic to stay still before you begin moving, honor that prompting.

- Spend some time dancing with that belief. Dance with this negativity, give this blockage its last turn on the dance floor, in the clear light of day. Just go with it, and notice what happens.

- Now you can make a powerful, healing choice, if you're willing. It's time to release this all-too-familiar partner; release this ugly, false belief about yourself that has been holding you back. Let the belief go. If it helps, make a gesture or body movement that, to you, represents letting go, and keep moving with that experience.

- You don't have to dance with that negative belief anymore! Let it go. It doesn't have to hold you down one moment longer.

- Whenever you feel as if you've let the belief go, come to a place of stillness and notice if a new belief has risen up in its place. Then, you may consider repeating the "Dancing with Our Positive Beliefs," page 76.

- If you feel as if you can't release the belief totally in one practice, that's okay—know that you haven't failed. I encourage you to take a moment in stillness and notice what you were able to let go of today, or simply congratulate yourself on giving the practice a try. You can always return to this practice at a different time to work through the other layers.

From Jamie's Music Box

- "Fantasie Impromptu" (Chopin) is a personal favorite of mine for this dance. It has many highs and lows, and the final section sounds like a breath of fresh air, the victorious renewal of coming to life.

- "Für Elise" (Beethoven)

- "Clair de Lune" (Debussy)

- "Blues for Klook" (Eddy Louiss) or similar pieces

- "Redemption Song" (Bob Marley) or similar pieces

- Any rendition of Leonard Cohen's "Hallelujah" or similar pieces

Since most of us carry multiple negative beliefs, there are many opportunities to incorporate this dance in our personal practice. Let go of any pressure to dance through all your negative beliefs during the course of one practice.

Nonstriving and self-compassion are both important when it comes to this particular practice. Even if you've done intensive therapeutic work to overcome the shame that these beliefs may cause, we all run the risk of having them come up in the wake of various life stressors. Thus, if "I'm not good enough" is a belief you've worked on before and you're identifying it today, be kind to yourself. None of us has positive thoughts about ourselves at all times, especially since the flow of life inevitably brings us stressors and wounds. Emotional charge and negative self-learning typically accompany these experiences. Returning to the practice again and again can foster deep healing and transformation.

Launching Out: Sharing the Practice with Others and Deepening Your Personal Practice

The key to adapting these practice suggestions for group settings is to know your audience. If you are considering facilitating the "Dancing with Our Negative Beliefs" practice, evaluate whether or not your group seems to be ready for it. If you are not sure, perhaps you'll choose to keep the focus on manifesting positive beliefs or "faking it 'til you make it." These practices are still very powerful in and of themselves.

Timing is also important. If you are going to use any of the facilitations offered in this chapter, they are best implemented in the middle portion of the class. Allow for safety and trust to develop between the group and the facilitator in the beginning of the class. As a personal preference, I facilitate practices like "Dancing with Negative Beliefs" in concert with the element of spirit, covered in the next chapter, and I provide an extended description of this fusion in chapter 7.

Another way I work directly with the mind when I facilitate is to incorporate certain reminders. I specifically challenge participants to think about, consider, or be mindful of a segment of their practice or one of the other elements. Here are some examples:

- Draw your attention to your _____ [breath, body, what you are hearing, natural sense of percussion].

- As you move, think about the idea of _____ [release, letting go, curiosity, acceptance, grace, love, joy, healing, beginner's mind].

- On this _____ [stretch, movement, song], be mindful of _____ [your breath, your muscles, your face].

- Think back to the intention that you set for yourself at the beginning of your practice today. What are you noticing now?

See where I'm going with this? Activating this purposeful awareness can teach you what is serving you and what seems to be working against you at any given moment. From there, you can experiment and make adjustments. You can learn how to become more responsive, instead of reactive. In psychological circles, we sometimes refer to this phenomenon as "retraining the brain." In class settings, the facilitator plants the seed. The practitioners take it where they need to go.

In personal practice, you may find this difficult to achieve without verbal reminders. Working with a guide, like the *Dancing Mindfulness: LIVE* recording (see page 185), may help you get started. Alternatively, if you've allocated a space for dancing mindfulness practice in your home, write down some of the facilitation lines offered in the book on sticky notes and place them around your space. At certain points in your practice, be sure to look up at the notes and follow the prompt of whatever note catches your eye. As I've suggested in other chapters, you can also record these statements on your phone or another device to keep playing during your practice. These steps may not be necessary the more familiar you become with asking yourself such questions. Know that these suggestions can be taken if you need them; everyone needs reminders, especially when you're just getting started.

Weaving It All Together

Opportunities for deeper healing emerge in any dancing mindfulness practice. In the early years of *Dancing Mindfulness*, I conducted a study on the first group of people to practice *Dancing Mindfulness* in a public setting.[7] This first group was primarily women, ages eighteen to sixty-one, from a variety of personal and professional backgrounds. Several of the participants revealed issues of mental illness, including anxiety, depression, postpartum depression, post-traumatic stress disorder, and addiction. From our open-ended questionnaire, I learned that through a dancing mindfulness practice, most participants experienced some kind of improvement in the emotional or spiritual domains. Participants reported feelings of happiness, empowerment, and acceptance; positive changes to self; and catharsis and release. As one participant noted, "I have experienced some powerful emotions during classes and learned that I could honor, accept, and release these emotions, rather than trying to escape from them, bury them, or brood over them." Said another participant:

> My favorite thing about this practice is that it is perfectly fine to tell your story, release the negative, and take in the positive and necessary energy through movement and music where and how you need it without so much as a word. It's the time in my busy week to be able to express my inner feelings without words.

Experiences in dancing mindfulness practice differ from person to person, and this diversity is especially pronounced in the element of the mind. As we discussed throughout this chapter, there are multiple ways to conceptualize the mind, and defining it can spark heated philosophical debate. Each tradition views the mind in its own way, and we all seem to have our own concepts of what constitutes the mind. As a result, practitioners take their work with this element to a variety of places. If you believe that you can't possibly practice with the element of the mind because of self-doubts or preconceived notions that you have about meditation, work with one of the other elements instead. They are all related to the mind somehow. Aristotle expressed this teaching when he said, "The energy of the mind is the essence of life."[8] May we learn to trust this energy in our journey to this present moment and may this journey enrich our entire life.

Try This: Mind, the Seven Attitudes, and the Creative Arts

The energy of the mind is the essence of life.

Do I embrace my mind as the essence of my life, or does doing this seem odd or even scary?

How might mindfulness practice help me to befriend my own mind?

- Consider the seven foundational attitudes of mindfulness practice: nonjudging, patience, beginner's mind, trust, nonstriving, acceptance, letting go.

- How does each attitude relate to mind? Consider saying each attitude out loud or spelling it out on a piece of paper and notice what happens. You can be still with the response or move with it.

- How can working with the mind help you to further develop these seven attitudes for your optimal health and well-being?

I encourage you to use dance, or any of the other creative arts, to contemplate these questions—get out your journal, your paints, your pencils, your camera—whatever helps you enter this place of contemplation. Perhaps you are a songwriter, a poet, or a fiction writer. Consider these channels to help you dance with the questions. Notice the connections that rise up when you fuse the practice of dancing mindfulness with any of your other practices or creative pursuits.

Other Voices on the Mind

Kashdan, Todd, and Joseph Ciarrochi. *Mindfulness, Acceptance, and Positive Psychology: The Seven Foundations of Well-Being*. Oakland, CA: Context Press, 2013.

Katie, Byron. *Your Inner Awakening: The Work of Byron Katie—Four Questions That Will Transform Your Life*. New York: Simon & Schuster, 2007.

Keeney, Bradford. *Shaking Medicine: The Healing Power of Ecstatic Movement*. Merrimac, MA: Destiny Publishers, 2007.

Shapiro, Francine. *Getting Past Your Past: Self-Help Strategies from EMDR Therapy*. Emmaus, PA: Rodale Books, 2013.

Siegel, Daniel. *The Mindful Brain: Reflection and Attunement in the Cultivation of Well-Being*. New York: W.W. Norton & Co., 2007.

Chapter 5

Spirit

The Greatness Guiding Our Dance

I love you when you bow in your mosque, kneel in your temple, pray in your church. For you and I are sons of one religion, and it is the spirit.

—*Kahlil Gibran*, The Prophet

A meaningful way in which I connect to the God of my understanding is to crank up some spiritual music and let it guide my dance. Music from my own Catholic-Christian background, and music from other faith and spiritual traditions, all resonate within my heart. Although I have plenty of Gregorian chant, kirtan, African-American spirituals, and Native American flute music in my collection, sometimes my most profound spiritual connections to music occur when I hear the messages of faith in show tunes or popular music. Dance is a powerful form of prayer for me. Simply defined, prayer is a channel of communication with my concept of the Divine, and my dance can express what words or thoughts simply cannot.

When my ex-husband moved out of our house shortly before our divorce, the room that was his office proved to be a beautiful, empty space I had available for dancing my prayers. Night after night I would put together spiritual playlists and just move with them, allowing tears to well up in my dance. One practice really stands out to me. I was listening to a song about Abraham and his consternation at the thought of sacrificing his son, Isaac. As I absorbed this musical rendering of Abraham's story, a flood of tears overwhelmed me in the midst of my movement. I came to the ground in one of the most powerful releases I ever experienced. Once the tears passed, calm suffused me, and I was able to trust the God of my understanding in a newer, deeper way.

It is impossible to offer a concise definition of *spirit* that will work for every reader of this book. Our conceptualizations of spirit and spirituality are individualized and open to interpretation, based on our own lived experiences. Because the laws of nature and science cannot generally explain the spiritual realm, coming up with a precise description becomes even more difficult. The most all-encompassing definition I can provide is this: *spirit is that which is greater than you or I.* Spirituality is our lived practice of honoring and connecting with that greatness, whether it be a deity, a series of deities, the cosmos, Mother Earth, the collective power of a group in practice, that inexplicable spark that dwells within us, or any combination of these manifestations. I strive to honor all spiritual paths that fundamentally serve the greater good. As an interfaith poster I saw once declared, "All truly spiritual paths meet in the middle." This sentiment essentially represents my position on what I consider to be *spirituality for the greater good.* I also believe that someone does not necessarily have to be religious in order to be spiritual, and I recognize that, for many, religious practices allow for connection with spirit.

Mindfulness practice is compatible with many paths, both spiritual and religious. Mindfulness meditation has origins in Buddhist meditation, yet there is nothing about it that's distinctively Buddhist. Some purists believe that to truly practice mindfulness, the core of the original Buddhist teachings must be followed. This rigidity has never worked for me along any spiritual path. I don't find it necessary to accept traditional Buddhism in order to practice mindfulness in daily living. Although I take an integrated approach to spirituality, I primarily identify as a Christian. In my experience, mindfulness practice is wonderfully compatible with Christianity. Friends of other faith traditions have shared similar sentiments with me about this compatibility with their religious paths. The practice of mindfulness simply calls us to become more aware in the present moment. The by-product of practice is cultivation of attitudes like trust, acceptance, letting go, and patience. Mindfulness practice heightened my awareness of Christ's message, strengthened my relationship with God, and taught me what being a Christian really means. If you are the type of Christian, Jew, Muslim, Hindu, or member of another religion who is open-minded enough to learn from the practices of other global cultures, I applaud you for having this attitude of non-judgment. My hope is that you will benefit from the practice of dancing mindfulness.

Dance: The Conduit of Spirit

Practices and teachings from the world's great faith traditions further our insight into the role of dance as a vehicle for connecting with spirit. When I consider some of these associations between dance and spirit, I am filled with gratitude that my personal dancing mindfulness practice gives me a chance to experience them for myself. Rabbi Miriam Maron, a dancer and psychotherapist, describes dance and movement as healing arts in Judaism. She writes:

> The word for dance and the word for illness, taught Rebbe Nachman of Breslov, are related: *ma'cho'l* for dance, *machah'lah* for illness or affliction. Not by accident do they both share the same root. After all, dancing brings one to a state of joy, and when the body is in a state of joy, the negative energies contributing to illness begin to dissipate.[1]

Many verses in the Hebrew Bible describe dance as a way to express gratitude to God. There are several psalms of this nature, although a verse from Exodus is especially descriptive: "Then Miriam the prophetess, the sister of Aaron, took a tambourine in her hand, and all the women went out after her with tambourines and dancing" (Exodus 15:20). In his reflection on King David's dance before the tabernacle, Rabbi Adam Jacobs remarks:

> In David's case, the dance was a vehicle for him to access deeper recesses of his consciousness. Like other repetitive acts such as mantras, prayer and meditation, the dancing overrides analytical consciousness, opening a purer and deeper channel. In this regard, dancing and praying may be considered very closely related (when done properly) and is the reason that many mystically inclined religious groups, such as Judaism's Hasidim, employ so much singing and dancing in their observance.[2]

Similar themes appear in texts and traditions from a variety of world cultures. Summarizing a plethora of global research on dance in her book *Dance—The Sacred Art*, Cynthia Winton-Henry explains:

> At the beginning of nearly every culture, dance arose at the foundation of collective spiritual life. Just as inconceivable as separating out deities and goddesses from everyday activities, dancing was intrinsic to the religiosity of indigenous groups. It could not be extricated. It was manna, daily bread. More than mere expression, dancing served as a primary means of knowing and creating the world. It carried technologies of healing, entertainment, and most definitely praying.[3]

For me, the whirling dervish is one of the great iconic representations of culture, dance, and prayer intersecting. Founded in the fourteenth century in the footsteps of Rumi, the Mevlevi Order within Sufism adopted the practice of whirling or spinning as a form of prayer to God. The order regards whirling as an active form of meditation. This tradition provides magnificent context for the Sufi proverb: God respects us when we work, but he loves us when we dance.

Native American spiritual teachings also offer treasure troves of wisdom about the power of dance. Dr. Carl Hammerschlag's best-selling memoir, *The Dancing Healers: A Doctor's Journey of Healing with Native Americans*, helped me deepen my own dancing mindfulness practice. His candid witness of how dance transformed him from academic and rigid to more holistic and spiritual inspired me to stay the course of sharing dance as a healing art with others. Hammerschlag, who was trained as a psychiatrist at Yale, reveals that when he first traveled to Arizona to work with the Indian Health Services, he believed he was bringing a wealth of knowledge about the human brain to a backward people. He quickly discovered that they had more to teach him about healing than he could ever teach them. He tells a particularly touching story of a tribal elder who, after listening to Dr. Hammerschlag's credentials, asked him if he could dance. To appease him, the doctor did a little shuffle by his bedside. The elder chuckled, replying, "You must be able to dance if you are to heal people."

Gabrielle Roth, founder of the 5Rhythms practice, is regarded as the mother of the modern conscious dance movement. In her own writing and teaching, she often intoned the indigenous teaching called the fourfold way. As explained by Dr. Angeles Arrien:

> Healers throughout the world recognize the importance of maintaining or retrieving the four universal salves: storytelling, singing, dancing, and silence. Shamanic societies believe that when we stop singing, stop dancing, are no longer enchanted by stories, or become uncomfortable with silence, we experience soul loss, which opens the door to discomfort and disease. The gifted healer restores the soul through use of the healing salves.[4]

Gabrielle Roth's classic book *Sweat Your Prayers* was another key piece of my own journey into conscious dance practice. A major theme of her book, and her work in general, is that Gabrielle didn't want to just dance. Through her dance she wanted to find God. In an article written shortly before her death, Gabrielle noted:

> Prayer is moving. Prayer is offering our bones back to the dance. Prayer is letting go of everything that impedes our inner silence. God is the dance and the dance is the way to freedom and freedom is our holy work.[5]

In this chapter, I will share some of the ways that the element of spirit—that which is greater than you or I—can be folded into the practice of dancing mindfulness. You can take the practices we've already covered and adapt them with the intention of connecting with spirit. I also honor your right not to use this element in your dancing mindfulness practice, or to adapt it in your own way. As a reminder, all spiritual paths that lead to the greater good are honored and valued in dancing mindfulness. If something that you read in this chapter doesn't resonate with your spiritual or religious belief system, feel free to take what you like and leave the rest. To demonstrate the wide range of variability and adaptability of practicing with this element, I even share the story of a *Dancing Mindfulness* facilitator who identifies as an atheist. She offers her experience of how she is able to incorporate the element of spirit into her practice.

Setting Sail with Personal Practice

For personal practice in this area, consider the notion of "dancing your prayers." My basic instruction: bring something to your heart—a petition, a sense of gratitude, an exultation—and then just go with it. Allow your prayer to be expressed through your movements. You may choose to do this in silence or with music. If you wish to move deeply into this area of practice, I suggest making a playlist of music that speaks to you spiritually. You will be amazed at what will unfold when you let yourself dance to this music.

Try This: Dancing with the Divine

Now that we have danced with our breath, our heartbeat, the sounds around us, and our bodies, it's time, if you are willing, to connect with spirit.

- For this dance, I invite you to call upon any element that you define as living in the realm of spirit. Ask spirit to be with you as you move more deeply into your practice.

- Look up to the heavens, look around you, look below you to the earth. Notice where your spiritual guide comes from. This guide may be your Higher Power, the God of your understanding, a healing shaman, the greater presence of the universe, or just the collective energy you absorb from being around your support system.

- Identify that guide and allow it to connect with your sense of spirit, as if your guide were leading the dance and you were following.

- Let your guide lead the dance, and notice where it takes you. Just notice where you go, without judgment.

From Jamie's Music Box

- "Hinei Ma Tov" (Holy Taya/Holly Shere)

- "Shalom Niggun" (One Love Devotional Chant)[6]

- "Doubting Thomas" (Chris Thile/Nickel Creek)

- "Ashoakan Farewell" (Jay Ungar/Molly Mason)

- "Journey Blind" (Jamie Marich)

- Instrumental versions of classic pop or rock songs can work nicely; "My Guitar Gently Weeps" and "Don't Stop Believing" are two of my favorites.

"Dancing with the Divine" can open you up to even deeper letting-go work. You may want to practice the "Dancing with the Divine" exercise (page 93) before "Dancing with Our Negative Beliefs" (page 80). I find the combination powerful. Think about some ways that you can blend these spirit questions into your practice. For instance:

- Ask your Higher Power to help show you this trap, this block that's been holding you back.

- Confronting your mental blocks, dancing with them, may be scary. Invite your Higher Power to guide the dance and help you through this process.

- As you breathe, consider your breath as a vehicle to invite in the Divine, allowing the body, mind, and spirit to come together. Notice what happens.

- Your Higher Power, your Divine, your sense of what's greater than you can help you let go ... let go ... let go ... release.

If you regularly work with shamanic principles, incorporating those into your dancing mindfulness practice or classes may be a good fit. My favorite working definition of shamanism comes from Dr. Michael Harner, founder of the Foundation for Shamanic Studies:

> The word "shaman" in the original Tungus language refers to a person who makes journeys to non-ordinary reality in an altered state of consciousness ... shamanism underlay all the other spiritual traditions on the planet, and the most distinctive feature of shamanism—but by no means the only one—was the journey to other worlds in an altered state of consciousness. Shamans are often called "see-ers" (seers), or "people who know" in their tribal languages, because they are involved in a

system of knowledge based on firsthand experience. Shamanism is not a belief system. It's based on personal experiments conducted to heal, to get information, or do other things.[7]

Since there is a strong tendency to associate shamanism with Native American folklore, music, and symbols, many practitioners of dancing mindfulness choose to invoke them in their dance. As Kirsten Koenig, my sister facilitator and a member of the Blackfoot nation, cautions, it is important to have an understanding of the cultural intent of these dances if you are going to use them.

Kirsten adapted a dance from her Native American tradition for a *Dancing Mindfulness* group. The dance calls for identifying negative blocks and then invoking the element of water, referred to as the "first medicine" in many nations, to clear the negativity.

Try This: Water, the First Medicine Dance

This dance is twofold, generally involving two songs. In the first part, use your hands, your feet, or both as if they were writing implements. In the second part of the dance, call upon imaginary water to rush through the space like a healing river. Many songs are perfect for this purpose—Victoria Shaw's "The River," made popular by Garth Brooks, and the spiritual "Wade in the Water" are two of my favorites. Allow this water and the practice of dancing with it to work in you, and if you are facilitating a group, encourage that process. Let the water wash away your doubts and create a new, transformative dance for your life.

- Cue up your first song and begin by making a list of the roadblocks in your life. Use nothing but your body—specifically, your feet and hands—to help you make this list.

- As spirit moves you, begin using your feet to trace into the earth all the things that are holding you back—words that represent what no longer serves you. Maybe it's fear, maybe it's doubt. Don't censor it, just use your foot to start writing. Let a dance unfold from these motions.

- When it feels organic, begin to use your hands to continue writing what is coming up into the open space around you. Allow the sharing of that list with the open space to also unfold into a dance.

- Perhaps you even want to take your visualized list onto the walls of your space. Continue writing, or if it feels better for you, draw images with your hands that represent what no longer serves you. Just notice what happens.

- At this point, transition to your second song. Now that we've given this work to our space, to the universe, I'd like you to imagine that a beautiful, healing river is beginning to flow through this space. This is not the kind of river that can drown you or hurt you. It's the kind of river that purifies and cleanses.

- Let that river wash away the lists you created in this space, and let the healing flow through you. Dance with it. Move with it.

Whenever you encourage release, especially of a deep nature, it is important to invoke some type of element to clear the energy that's been released. Something I've learned from my friendship with Kirsten is that just "dancing stuff out" can create some weird energy floating around the room if what's been danced out has nowhere to go. Kirsten's suggestion of invoking the water imagery is a great example of how to clear the space. In some people's belief systems, the idea of sending what's released up to the heavens works well. Invoking the imagery of fire to transform what's been released into smoke, and then sending that smoke to the heavens also works. In the earlier days of my dancing mindfulness practice, I focused a great deal on fire imagery, although in more recent times I've become a bigger fan of sending any released negativity back to the earth. As my reiki master Valerie Spitaler shared with me, passing on the Native American wisdom of her teacher, "Mother Earth loves absorbing energy, of whatever kind. It's like chocolate to her. Release the unwanted energy to her, because she has the power to transform it into something else." Although I received this wisdom as part of my reiki training, the applications to dancing mindfulness practice are obvious to me. Thus, at the end of dancing mindfulness practices (both personal and in a group setting), I invite any unwanted negativity or energy that's lingering in the space to be returned to Mother Earth.

Whatever spiritual focus is genuine for you, I encourage you to weave it into your dancing mindfulness practice. Perhaps it is shamanism, energy work, or yoga; maybe it is a more religious focus, like Christianity, Judaism, Buddhism, or Hinduism. Lead with what feels natural to you. In group settings, issue invitations to connect, and avoid making demands. People respond much better to invitations. Remember that mindfulness meditation is not a religion; it can be practiced alongside any spiritual path, and dancing mindfulness practice is no exception.

Launching Out: Sharing the Practice with Others and Deepening Your Personal Practice

I am honored that many practitioners refer to *Dancing Mindfulness* classes as spiritual, and I certainly recognize that spirit may be the primary element that jumps out for such participants. As Kirsten Koenig observes: "It is impossible for me to dance without tapping into spirit." I share her sentiments. However, this phenomenon may not be true for everyone. Recognizing people's potential discomfort with bringing spirit into their dance is important, especially if you're facilitating a group that's not specifically billed as a gospel-themed or religious-themed *Dancing Mindfulness* group. For some practitioners, even if they are spiritual or religious, the idea of using dance to connect with spirit may be radical or foreign, and, as a result, initially uncomfortable. There are ways to facilitate with spirit without shoving it down people's throats.

The biggest barrier I've observed in connecting to spirit with dance is when someone has a history of being battered by previous experiences with religion or spirituality. In our discussions about abuse, we generally think of physical, emotional, or sexual wounding, yet we fail to consider the power of spiritual abuse. Spiritual abuse is a real phenomenon. Spiritual abuse is when a person, an institution (that is, a church or a religious community), or a government entity uses God or religion as a tool to gain power and control. Although spiritual abuse encompasses the wounding that people experience in cults or at the hands of sexually exploitative priests and ministers, its manifestations are often more subtle. Think of people who internalize a great deal of shame about who they are— sexually, emotionally, or constitutionally—because of messages they've heard in church or received in their home of origin. You may even identify as one of these individuals. Consider those with "black and white" faith because their religious communities preach that commitment to that particular faith or path is an "all-or-nothing" proposition. Think about people who believe God is punishing them because of something they did or didn't do; these are typically beliefs instilled by abusive systems.

Dancing mindfulness is a practice that honors where you are coming from and invites you to embrace your own conceptualization of spirituality. The practice also respects that if you are happy with your existing religion or spiritual practice, you do not have to abandon it. Although I generally don't make a big statement about this duality at the beginning of a class, when I do segue into a more spiritual place (usually at the transition between the beginning and the middle of class), I make sure to deliver lines like these:

- If you are open to it, we are going to journey to a spiritual place.

- All paths of spirituality that lead to a greater good are honored here. Consider the path that you are currently on as we continue to dance.

- Allow whatever you believe is greater than you to enter your dance, to connect with your spirit.

- What is happening in your spirit at this point? Just take a moment and tune in.

These lines can be used at any point in the guided practice, at your discretion, and you can blend them with other elements. If you are reading this book primarily for your own personal practice, you can incorporate these suggestions into your own practice.

In 12-step programs, those who cannot conceive of a Higher Power in the form of a divinity may use the fellowship of people gathered for wellness as their Higher Power. Some people in Alcoholics Anonymous even refer to G.O.D. as "group of drunks." There is something to this idea. Even if the idea of a Divine is too hurtful to you or not within your grasp, you can still be spiritual if you can see the collective energy generated by the group as a force greater than you, existing outside of your individual self. To many people in self-help groups and other fellowships, the power of the group can be very healing.

Becky Bright, a *Dancing Mindfulness* facilitator based in Denver, identifies as an atheist. She even sports a large tattoo on her arm that she calls her "losing my religion" ink—a piece representative of her journey with spiritual abuses that ultimately led her to where she is today. What is curious to me about Becky is how she continues to dance fully and vigorously during practices that involve spiritual songs, even our popular dance chapel sessions, which we hold during facilitator trainings and retreats (more on dance chapel later in the chapter). I once asked Becky how she does this, and her answer was simple: the group. It's the collective energy and joy of the group dancing together to these types of songs that moves her.

Becky explains:

Dancing mindfulness has opened up a new path to my own inner workings. One does not have to rely on a spiritual consciousness or journey (or religiosity) to benefit from what dancing mindfulness seeks to provide. What dance chapel gives is directly proportional to what the individual can get from it. Sometimes a song or a certain movement shows the dancer that they are their own deity; they have their own center point from which their interpersonal power and strength can be derived. It can be completely internal, yet awakened by something external (a song or a piece of music). The community one can experience by dancing in the presence of others is very powerful. Even if you don't know the other participants, the moments when we gaze at each other's feet without judgment, then slowly work our way to eye contact (if it feels right, while honoring your experience), can create community and a sense of togetherness among the dancers.... When we think of "church," many times there is pressure to conform to a certain way of behaving or, at least, having to convince people that everything in life is lining up perfectly or meeting the church community's expectations. There are no such restrictions when you dance for yourself in an environment where you can feel anything that arises within you and express those feelings through the freedom of movement.

Creating Connections

Because the power of the group can have such profound spiritual implications, I enjoy promoting connection with practitioners in *Dancing Mindfulness* classes. Typically, when the tempo of the music starts to pick up, you'll find that people will naturally connect with each other. If I don't see this happening, I'll issue invitations for participants to make eye contact with one another, or to reach out, grab someone's hand, and take that person for a whirl. My greatest caution here is to keep safety in mind. Too much interpersonal connection before the group has had time to gel and, quite frankly, feel safe with each other, can be intimidating. I like to lead with lines like these: "If you like, take a partner. If you don't want to partner with anyone, just continue moving." A connection suggestion that I picked up along the way in my visits to conscious dance classes at yoga retreat centers is to first begin by having people notice the feet dancing around them. If looking at feet feels okay, then you can invite your group to move up and look at knees, then shoulders, and then, if they are comfortable, eyes. If I see that people are reasonably comfortable making eye contact, I will invite them to extend a hand if they are comfortable with being touched for a simple hand-to-hand connection. I say publicly that if you don't wish to be touched, simply put your hand to your heart as a signal of opting out, and you will not be judged for it.

I tend to encourage direct interpersonal connection after the middle section of the class, after people feel more at ease with themselves in relation to the space and to each other. One of my favorite ways to do this is to invite people to come into a circle after a Runway Dance (page 57) or another dance of empowerment. I like to have the group hold hands; you can give people the option of being outside the circle. Songs like the classic "Can You Feel the Love Tonight?" by Elton John (from *The Lion King*) are a perfect backdrop for facilitation that encourages swaying or moving with the energy of the group. You can also suggest a fun twist on this exercise using tunes such as the Beatles' "All Together Now." If you have any type of folk dancing background, feel free to use one of the circle or line dances that you know. Sometimes teaching a good old classic grapevine step or T-A-N-G-O tango step (available at www.dancingmindfulness.com/resources) does the trick. I teach the step, usually in a circle or line, and then, after people seem to get it, I invite open exploration of the space with the new step.

Another lively group facilitation that can promote connection is a variation on the classic game of Follow the Leader. Invite your class to come down to one end of the room. As the facilitator, be the first to demonstrate, coming up with your impromptu moves as the music directs you and inviting the mass of people behind you to follow along. I generally say something like this: "You don't have to copy me exactly, just be inspired by the movement." Then, when the group reaches the other end of the room, I invite someone else to jump out and lead, and we keep doing this until the song or series is over. Some people are hesitant to participate in this and that's okay, but those who like to take their turn leading tend to come up with some creative twists. From my experience, there is great spiritual power in a group of people moving together in creative synchrony. Also, this dance gives you a perfect opportunity to use popular, upbeat music. In most of my classes, I like to work in at least one or two of these songs.

Another option for promoting the spiritual experience of a group moving in communion is to set up what we've come to call a "dance chapel." In dance chapel, there is no verbal facilitation—the music on the playlist is the only facilitation. You can put the playlist together to create a desired effect. At trainings and retreats, we specify a starting time for dance chapel on the door and ask for the sacredness of the space to be respected as people enter. When I offer dance chapel in the morning on trainings and retreats, I start with very earthy, ambient music to promote seated connection, breathwork, and other necessary stretching. I then build the flow of the music to eventually get people up on their feet and energized for the day. It's not uncommon for dance chapels to start with the soft sounds of a gently moving stream, work up to gospel ballads, and then end with something highly charged like George Michael's "Faith" or MC Hammer's "Pray."

Essentially, you are putting together a playlist and setting the intention for sacred space when you opt for the dance chapel style of dancing mindfulness. I put together dance chapel as a shorter version of the dance church experience that I had at Esalen. I coined the term *dance chapel* to suggest the shorter duration and "drop in" quality of the experience. For the first dance chapel I hosted, I used all spiritually themed pieces of music from various traditions because it was a Sunday, and that tradition has stuck with our facilitator trainings and retreats. In constructing dance chapel playlists for personal practice, you can stay with this vibe or use songs that reflect your own sense of spirituality.

My biggest caution for going the dance chapel route is to use it with a group of people familiar with *Dancing Mindfulness* or other improvisational/conscious dance practices. If you are in a setting where any number of newcomers will enter and say, "What the heck are they all doing?" then opting for more traditional instructional facilitation is more appropriate. In the Thursday night community *Dancing Mindfulness* gathering in my home area of Youngstown, Ohio, if all the regulars show up, it is common for us to simply practice dance chapel. The practitioners are familiar with the process, so we (my rotating facilitators and I, that is) let them do their thing. However, if there is even one new person who comes on any given night, we go the route of standard facilitation instead.

Try This: Setting Up a Dance Chapel

- The key is to let the music do the facilitation—no verbal facilitation is required.

- What is your intent for the dance chapel? Do you want to run it like a standard *Dancing Mindfulness* class, where you start people on the ground, get them up to their feet, and bring them back down again? Or would you rather start them in a slow, grounding way, and then get them up on their feet in high energy to transition into the rest of the day? Whatever your intention, let the music help you craft it.

- Is your group aware of what you'll be doing? If you have a regular core of people who understand the purpose of "just going with it," you are all set. At some retreats, I put a sign on the door explaining the process or I offer a brief orientation the night before.

- As with other forms of *Dancing Mindfulness* group practice, be open to verbal processing either with the group or one-on-one after the session.

Weaving It All Together

Although my experiences with dance chapel began in group settings, it soon dawned on me that much of my personal practice could be described as a dance chapel. Because the element of spirit is a vital part of my personal practice, I now see every time that I intentionally dance as my own, private dance chapel. While I recognize that approaching practice this way might not work for everyone, consider whether it might resonate with you as you develop your personal practice.

Holly Speenburgh, a certified *Dancing Mindfulness* facilitator from New Jersey, regularly incorporates the dance chapel process into her personal practice. She lives near the beach in Asbury Park. After experiencing the dance chapel format during her own facilitator training, she decided to go to the beach at least once a week with a dance chapel–style playlist and engage with the fusion of music, her dance, and the elements of nature. Holly observes:

> *Dancing Mindfulness* has taught me how to let go of self-doubt and enjoy my emotional journey. I find myself often mentally preparing playlists for my own practice. My self-practice has helped me work my way through hard times and has allowed me to find the inner confidence I needed to pursue my graduate degree. Working on self-practice has allowed me to let go of my shoulds, coulds, woulds, and worrying about how I look. Doing my self-practice on the beach has been a huge part of this. It used to be that I would go early before anyone was there. As life got in the way of that, I released that worry, dancing and saying "screw it," regardless of who was there. I needed the water as much as the dance. I figured that, if they thought I was weird, they wouldn't talk to me anyway!

During this time of exploring her use of personal practice and the dance chapel format, Holly received a brutal rejection letter in response to her application to her first-choice graduate program in social work. The process of personal dancing mindfulness practice allowed Holly to work through this rejection and ultimately led her down another, more suitable path. She notes:

> When I was rejected from my first grad school, it was tough, yet I was doing solid self-practice two times a week and that gave me the persistence to keep going. The word *humanistic* became so important to me during this process, and it's ultimately what led me to the graduate school I'm in now. I went online and searched "humanistic" and "social work" and the program that I'm in now came up. In terms of goodness of fit, I couldn't have asked for anything better.

In my life journey and dancing mindfulness practice, I've come to appreciate spirit not only as that which is greater than you or I, but also as a force that allows for the awesome convergence of disparate pieces in a way that cannot be easily explained by the laws of science. Every time I hear Holly share her story I am reminded of this possibility. When I behold what Kirsten, who is admittedly very "spiritual," and Becky, who is admittedly not, have to say about their experiences with the spirit element in dancing mindfulness, I am struck by a sense of gratitude—gratitude for the convergence, gratitude for the process, gratitude for the diversity that characterizes spiritual practice. My own words cannot sufficiently express this gratitude, which typically means that something beyond my understanding or the laws of nature are at work. I find instead that to express this gratitude, I must dance it. I carry the words of Henri Nouwen, one of my great spiritual teachers, into my next dance:

> Perhaps nothing helps us make the movement from our little selves to a larger world than remembering God in gratitude. Such a perspective puts God in view in all of life, not just in the moments we set aside for worship or spiritual disciplines. Not just in the moments when life seems easy.[8]

Try This: Spirit, the Seven Attitudes, and the Creative Arts

The dance of gratitude nourishes the dance of life.

How can I express my gratitude for spirit in my dance today?

Is there anything keeping me from accessing spirit in this present moment?

- Consider the seven foundational attitudes of mindfulness practice: nonjudging, patience, beginner's mind, trust, nonstriving, acceptance, letting go.

- How does each attitude relate to your conceptualization of spirit? Consider simply breathing or organically moving with each attitude and notice what happens. You can be still with the response or move with it.

- How can working with your conceptualization of spirit help you further develop these seven attitudes for your optimal health and well-being?

I encourage you to use dance, or any of the other creative arts, to contemplate these questions—get out your journal, your paints, your pencils, your camera—whatever helps you enter this place of contemplation. Perhaps you are a songwriter, a poet, or a fiction writer. Consider these channels to help you dance with the questions. Notice the connections that rise up when you fuse the practice of dancing mindfulness together with any of your other practices or creative pursuits.

Other Voices on Spirit

Arrien, Angeles. *The Four-Fold Way: Walking the Paths of the Warrior, Teacher, Healer, and Visionary*. New York: Harper-Collins, 2013.

Kramer, Joel, and Diana Alstad. *The Guru Papers: Masks of Authoritarian Power*. Berkeley, CA: Atlantic Books, 1993.

Nouwen, Henri. *The Dance of Life: Weaving Sorrows and Blessings into One Joyful Step*. Notre Dame, IN: Ave Maria Press, 2006.

Riley, Reba. *Post-Traumatic Church Syndrome: A Memoir of Humor and Healing in 30 Religions*. Atlanta: Chalice Press, 2015.

Roth, Gabrielle. *Sweat Your Prayers: Movement as Spiritual Practice*. New York: Tarcher, 1998.

Van Vonderen, Jeff, and David Johnson. *The Subtle Power of Spiritual Abuse: Recognizing and Escaping Spiritual Manipulation and False Authority Within the Church*. Bloomington, MN: Bethany House Publishers, 1991.

Winton-Henry, Cynthia. *Dance—The Sacred Art: The Joy of Movement as Spiritual Practice*. Woodstock, VT: SkyLight Paths Publishing, 2009.

Video Resource

- *Dancing with Monks and Mystics*, DVD from Abbey of the Arts. Available at www.abbeyofthearts.com.

Chapter 6

Story

Embracing Our Journey

The universe is made of stories, not of atoms.
—Muriel Rukeyser

I enjoy working in human services because I love a good story. Each of us has a unique story (or series of stories) about our life. Sharing those stories with others may prove to be a very healing experience. My love of stories, themes, and motifs is why I am drawn to qualitative research in my field. Large-scale research studies that attempt to quantify the human experience hold little appeal for me, especially considering that so much research in the social sciences is laboratory-contrived. My preference is for reading case studies and phenomenology, a qualitative method that seeks to describe the lived experience of a person or a group of people. I feel that I learn something about human beings reading such literature. Even in my own field, I champion the cause of qualitative research, although this often falls on deaf ears in the helping professions that have been so influenced by the medical model. People want to see things *measured* in linear and logical terms. There is nothing linear about the human experience.

Professionals who value artistic expression usually grasp this concept because we realize that the human experience is too complex to be measured in numbers or pigeonholed into scientific concepts. If I want to know about a client or a group, I listen to their story. I become fascinated with their story, because it is the primer for understanding their experience. Dancing mindfulness practice affords you an opportunity to share the intricacies of your story in a dynamic, potentially therapeutic way. You may find that in the process of sharing your story through this practice, you are able to embrace it, which can lead to a greater sense of self-acceptance and self-compassion. You may even use the practice to help you write a new ending for your story or manifest a renewed vision for your life's journey.

Healing in the Telling

Just as with dancing and drumming, cultures around the globe tap into the power of storytelling as a healing art, as they have since the dawn of time. In Western psychology, patients are typically encouraged to share their stories in some way, regardless of how the individual therapist practices therapy. Twelve-step groups encourage members to share their experience, strength, and hope at meetings. In my part of the country, we often get a whole forty-five minutes to share our story with a group. On the power of telling one's story, esteemed social worker and recovery writer Dr. Brené Brown asserted, "If we can share our story with someone who responds with empathy and understanding, shame can't survive."[1]

Non-Western cultures have long recognized the healing power of storytelling. This does not necessarily have to be literal. For instance, in many East African cultures, it is considered taboo to talk about trauma experiences. However, it is acceptable for a person to process emotion by sharing the story of her experience in the form of an allegory, creating a new ending that speaks to the survivor spirit. In African cultures and in other places around the globe, healing is achieved by visiting a village elder and hearing the stories of experience shared by that elder. The folk story canon of most global cultures contains striking themes of overcoming trauma-laden adversity through ritual, community, or a combination of the two. Tales such as "The Tiger's Whisker" (Korea) and the "Myth of Tyr" (Old Norse) are powerful examples of folk stories that craft a template for healing.

The faith traditions cited throughout this book all contain a rich bounty of stories used to communicate the teachings of the faith. Marilyn McFarlane curated a lovely anthology of these stories for children in her book *Sacred Stories*. Even as an adult I find this collection appropriate for those of us willing to cultivate the curiosity and beginner's mind of a child. As a child growing up in the Judeo-Christian tradition, I loved the stories in the Bible more than anything else. The story of Joseph and his brothers from the Hebrew Bible spoke to my mystical spirit, beginning my fascination with dream interpretation. In the Christian gospels, I was captivated by Jesus teaching in parables. Looking back on my experience of listening to these stories, I realize that Jesus's use of the story showed me a combination of his compassion, his humanity, and his recognition that storytelling, not just raw preaching, is a most artful way to impart sacred teachings.

Owning, Embracing, Sharing

Whether you are listening to others' stories or telling your own, the art of the story holds great healing potential. Reading, listening to, or witnessing others share their stories inspires me. A story of personal experience and works of fiction or reinterpretation of others' stories fuel me with the courage to tell my own stories and ultimately accept those stories as a part of me. We sometimes refer to this act of self-acceptance as "owning our story." Katherine Preston, whose autobiography *Out with It* details her journey of growing up with a severe stutter, defines owning your story as follows:

> There is no harm in speaking about the pieces of ourselves that
> we are proud of, and yet doing so does little more than inflate

our own egos. The more powerful part of "owning" our story is speaking about those pieces that make us feel embarrassed or ashamed. Bringing our greatest weaknesses out of the closet and into the spotlight. If we are lucky, there is a certain catharsis in doing so, the sense of a burden being lifted.[2]

In speaking with many of my friends about the idea of owning one's story, I recognized that this phrase doesn't work for everyone. In many Buddhist meditation traditions, teachers will caution you not to remain attached to your story lines, especially those that are rigidly defined or contribute to your sense of feeling stuck. Remember the negative belief traps that we covered in chapter 4, on the element of mind? All of those correspond to a story line or a series of story lines. Buddhist teacher Robert Altobello explains how this works:

> We draw a storyline around our *experience*, and the limitations of those storylines make us feel caged, as if there were no other possible way to experience the present moment. Mindfulness frees one from this cage by allowing one to experience the situation without these stifling conceptual boundaries—without the storyline animating the experience.[3]

If you make a similar connection, consider how you can use your dance as a way to come back to the present moment when those old negative beliefs, fueled by story, are caging you. Some days I use my personal dancing mindfulness practice in this way.

Other days my dancing mindfulness practice calls me to fully explore the story lines that ensnare me. My belief system on that matter closely parallels that of my primary spiritual teacher, *Dancing Mindfulness* facilitator, author, and Benedictine oblate Christine Valters Paintner. In her reflections on the desert mothers and fathers of early Christian monasticism, she writes: "Journeying toward God means showing up fully for our inner struggles, engaging with them fully, coming to terms with our wounds and inner divisions, and doing the hard, slow work of healing."[4] Reflecting on a passage like this, embracing my story, makes more sense to me than owning it. When I think of embracing the stories that form the collage of my own personal history, I see a picture of me giving myself a hug and accepting it all—the joy and the sorrow, the worthiness and the shame, what has been and what is yet to be. In embracing myself in this way, I embrace acceptance and self-compassion.

However you characterize the element of story—telling, owning, or embracing—you can work with it in dancing mindfulness practice. In this chapter, I will provide you with different practices and ideas to help you with this exploration.

Setting Sail with Personal Practice

By its very nature as an art, dance yearns to tell the story of people who claim their birthright to dance. Whether the dances are danced through historical vehicles of folk dance, choreographed performances, or the spontaneity of a conscious dance practice like dancing mindfulness, stories can be told, retold, and rewritten. Every moment of a dancing mindfulness practice provides an opportunity to tell a story. Even if you need to simply sit with an emotion instead of move with it during a moment of your dancing mindfulness experience, you are honoring your personal story in that moment. The act of sitting with or moving with an emotion, a bodily sensation, or any other experience may end up being a powerful component in writing a new ending for your story.

For fourteen years, I had the privilege of working part time or on a consultancy basis as a high school speech and debate coach. My specialty was working with students in the areas of prose and poetry reading, dramatic interpretation, and motivational speaking (original oratory). Through my own experiences in competitive speech in high school and working with dozens of brilliant students over the years, I realized that every facial movement, every hand gesture, every little nuance is a chance to deepen the impact of the story you are telling. In dancing mindfulness practice, too, the element of story magnifies the impact. We each have a unique story and simply entering into a practice session honors where we are at in that journey. The intention that you may set at the beginning of your practice comes with its own story. The dancing mindfulness experience gives you a chance to find a way to express your story or stories, some of which come from places of deeply held emotion that has never been allowed to see the light.

If you haven't done it before, the best place to start with such a process is to cue up a piece of music that consistently stirs up emotion in you, regardless of the genre. If you routinely sing along to songs in the car—I mean, really get into them so that others take notice—cue up that music. Set the intention of telling your story, then breathe in the music and just notice what happens. Be mindful that this doesn't have to be your full life story; it can simply be the story of your day or of one facet of your life. For example, "My intention is to dance the story of my faith" or "I will dance the chains of addiction off my body." The options are limitless.

A recovery practice from which I've derived great benefit over the years is making a gratitude list. I typically use a pen-to-paper journal for this process, as instructed by my first recovery sponsor, whom I met when working in Bosnia. Whenever I complained about some aspect of my life that I found disagreeable, especially when it came to things that would likely have no bearing on my life in a year's time—a disagreement with my boss, the snide comment a person directed my way—she challenged me to write out a gratitude list. The challenge was to be as specific as possible, including at least ten items. Although the gratitude items could be general—a car to get to work, a warm place to sleep at night—I usually found the lists most powerful when I could specify gratitude for the person or situation that challenged me. In personal dancing mindfulness practice, I often combine the two practices of gratitude lists and dance. After writing out a list, I may cue up some music and then dance the gratitude, either as a spontaneous expression of gratitude or by using the dance to act out each element on the list. Sometimes I need to dance first before I can write out the gratitude list. Gratitude is a marvelous theme to dance to, and there is no shortage of songs that celebrate this virtue. My personal favorites are Dido's "Thank You" and Sinead O'Connor's "Thank You for Hearing Me."

A dynamic practice can be simply challenging yourself to look deeply into your heart and tell your story to the dance floor, a process I've come to call storydancing. This can be the story of your whole life or the story of what you're living through right now. It can be the story of your day that's already passed. You may feel called to use this practice for the purpose of transformation and manifestation, allowing the dance to help create a new ending or usher in a new chapter. Many conscious dance forms make use of similar techniques, inspired by centuries of global traditions in both dance and storytelling.

Try This: Storydancing

Perhaps you've already explored dancing with your breath, your heart, your mind, your body, and your concept of spirit. Notice what's happening within you. I now invite you to allow all the elements to work together and create your story.

- Tell your story to the earth below you, the space around you.

- Your space is your canvas, your body is the paintbrush. Allow your story to be created in your space. The colors and the elements are being sent to you right now through your breath, through your spirit.

- Paint your story, create your story, dance your story in this space!

- You have options—it may feel organic to simply dance the story up to this present moment. If you believe that old story lines prevent you from experiencing the joy of the present moment, perhaps just notice those different story lines that pop up as you dance. Practice the challenge of noticing them, letting them go, and then returning to the present moment. If

> you feel inspired to move your story from this present moment
> and let the dance help you create a desired ending or a new,
> desired chapter in the journey, keep going with that process.

With storydancing, there are a variety of approaches you can take to the music. You can go instrumental, in which case you want to choose something with an emotionally evocative vibe. I personally enjoy using string quartet music here. Many instrumentals, both traditional and modern, nicely support the art of storytelling. Pieces with lyrics can also be an interesting choice, especially if you are dancing on a certain theme. Songs like Adele's "Rolling in the Deep" are excellent for dancing out stories of regret or pain in lost relationships. On one occasion when I took a conscious dance class at Kripalu, the facilitator used this song and I really got into it. I felt as if I sorted through three different relationship issues during that one dance! Typically there is something on the Top 40 list at any given time that can serve a similar purpose, or your own musical library may offer a piece that's even more appropriate for you.

From Jamie's Music Box

These are some of my favorite pieces of music for dancing mindfulness personal practice. They proved very powerful in helping me embrace parts of my own story at various times in my practice journey. I am listing them here along with some of the story themes they helped me bring to life.

- "Love Hurts" (Gram Parsons, various cover versions)/lost love

- "Tennessee Waltz" (multiple versions)/lost love

- "Mad World" (multiple versions)/pain, frustration of living

- "Across the Universe" (the Beatles, multiple versions)/ wandering, the story thus far

- "Colorful" (the Verve Pipe)/finding your own voice

- "Tomorrow Will Be Kinder" (The Secret Sisters, from *The Hunger Games* soundtrack)/hope for a brighter future

- "Defying Gravity" (from the *Wicked* soundtrack, multiple versions)/rising above adversity, acceptance of self

- "I Will Survive" (Gloria Gaynor, various cool cover versions)/ survival, overcoming hardship and trauma

Enrolling in Another's Story

In dancing mindfulness practice, you have a chance to tell your own stories or to take on another character's story for a while. You may discover that you can lose your inhibitions or work through emotional material more effectively when you are taking on a role. In the spirit of mindfulness, I challenge you to be totally present and aware in any role that you may assume. Maybe you wish to dance one of your favorite stories from sacred faith traditions or from the global canon of folktales. Consider choosing a piece of music from that faith tradition or from that culture for this experience. Maybe you are dancing a character from a movie or a musical that is special to you; consider dancing with music from that soundtrack.

Music from other eras may create a similar effect. For instance, cuing up a Glenn Miller big band classic or an old school MGM musical can bring out a wide array of characters. The music of the French chanteuse Edith Piaf holds a special place in my heart, and I also enjoy modern interpretations of music from her era by artists like Madeleine Peyroux. When I invite such music into my personal dancing mindfulness practice, I immediately begin to take on a different character. What makes this practice mindful for me is tapping into what that character can teach me about myself during this moment in my life's journey.

Mixing Media

Dancing the element of story in personal practice is much like writing in a journal, songwriting, or creating visual art. As many musicians and artists will tell you, we often create just for ourselves, for practice, for exploration, even if we never share the finished product in public. Think about writing in a journal. Do you share everything in it in public? Of course not! So think about your dancing mindfulness practice as a way to dance what you might normally write in your journal.

Counselor and *Dancing Mindfulness* facilitator Ramona Skriiko derives great benefit from the process of personal practice, expressing through dance what she can't quite put into a journal in words:

> I've discovered it's much easier to dance how I feel about danc-ing mindfulness than to put it into writing! I love participat-ing in a *Dancing Mindfulness* group, but my personal practice is when I get to give myself exactly what I need. It's a private time when I can focus on my emotions and my body. I get to spend time putting together a playlist of music I need to hear, music that will express whatever I might be struggling with or thinking about. I get to be mindful of all the feelings the music inspires in me and all the ways my body wants to move. I can notice things like the fact that my feet want to move more than usual and how that might relate to my need to move forward from a place where I've been stuck. I can cry or laugh or just explore the power and joy that I feel inside when I'm dancing. It's a different experience than when I'm dancing with a group. It's more personal and more intimate. Allowing my body to move in new ways within a group of other dancers can be extremely empowering; being fully present with myself during my personal practice has been healing on many levels.

Maybe you will find that engaging in personal dancing mindfulness practice fits better for you than simply writing in a journal. Or per-haps you will discover that engaging in personal dancing mindful-ness practice works in synchrony with other expressive art forms. This fusion may help you work with your story, however you may need to, and ultimately embrace it.

Try This: Telling Your Story in Dance and Poetry

After your next dance in personal practice, take a few moments to sit with your breath, centering in the stillness. Although you can take pen to paper and just notice what comes out, see if you can spend a few moments writing your own verses of poetry. There's no pressure for it to rhyme or even be perfect. Simply ask, What's the song of my experience in this moment?

Perhaps you can draw inspiration from one of our facilitators, Fonda Kingsley of Grand Rapids, Michigan. Her artistic name is Butterfli Journei.

> A unique journei, a journei to be shared by one, a
> journei that only I can go, a
>   journei of raw emotions unleashed.
>   Where my mind and body taps into with my soul
> and healing captures my heart—
>   without warning—without notice, the dance takes me
>   hostage ... like a butterfly in a cocoon ...
>   I AM TRANSFORMED ... no longer the same, I am
> set Free.

Combining a personal dancing mindfulness experience with other forms of creativity can inspire you in multiple ways. In addition to my experiences dancing, I discovered that songwriting offered me an effective medium for embracing my story. My albums *Under My Roof* and *Grace of a Woman* are collections of songs that I wrote as part of my own healing journey. Through songs like "Swallowed Glass" (from *Under My Roof*) I've been able to embrace the darkest experiences of my addiction:

> *Heal me from within, heal these wounds from glass I swallowed*
> *Though everything may seem alright, Lord I'm bleeding inside.*

Songs like "I Think I'll Let You" (from *Grace of a Woman*) help me share my story of how I experienced spiritual awakening. In this song, written within the first year of my sobriety and arranged for recording later, I express how my Higher Power (the *you* in this verse) turned the tide of my own personal history:

> *I can't, but you can, I think I'll let you*
> *Open up this door for me to freedom abounding*
> *I can't, you can, I think I'll let you*
> *Open up this door for love and joy awaiting*
> *With happiness and peace.*

In your next practice, keep a journal, sketchbook, canvas and paints, or your musical instrument accessible. After dancing, take a breath and just notice what comes up in the other media. Like Fonda, I also like to write poetry after I dance and simply be present with the process. You can also adapt this exercise to retreat or small group study experiences.

Once again, in the spirit of safety, seek support if your personal practice takes you to a place that is unexpected or scary. It is completely normal if dancing your story brings up distress. Just go with it, knowing that you can seek support if you need it or that you can revisit breath strategies for self-soothing. It can also be a solid safety practice to have a few of your sure-thing "happy" songs on deck to cue up if you need to come back to a more secure place. For years, I've kept some variation of a "happy song" playlist on my iPod. These selections lift my mood, no matter what my emotional state. If fully engaging with the ideas and practices described in this book appeals to you, consider making yourself such a playlist as a safety strategy. And cheesy eighties pop tunes are totally okay—those comprise about half of my happy playlist!

Launching Out: Sharing the Practice with Others and Deepening Your Personal Practice

If practitioners are willing and the venue is right, the *Dancing Mindfulness* experience also gives people a chance to share their stories in the group setting. There are simple facilitation lines you can use to attune people to the element of story and perhaps deepen the experience. These lines can be delivered as part of the general class flow. Later in the section, I offer some guidelines on how you can purposefully group people together. Consider how these questions might work in a group:

- What story are you telling with this movement?

- How can you share part of your story with this dance?

- Dance this story in a spirit of nonjudgment.

When I engage in personal practice, these lines work well for intention setting. Very often I set the intention for my personal practice like this: "Let this practice be a place where I can dance my story of today in a spirit of nonjudgment and nonstriving."

You can also incorporate props into your personal dancing mindfulness practice or group facilitation. For instance, many conscious dance forms I studied make use of scarves and, inspired by these forms, I often use scarves in my *Dancing Mindfulness* classes. Having just the right scarf can bring out a character in you or help you connect to a hidden dimension of yourself. For me, a scarf I choose from a pile can give me the feeling of having wings, which represents the release of inhibitions in my movement. Mary Lynne Zahler, a *Dancing Mindfulness* facilitator in Akron, Ohio, introduced our group to the use of miniature, color-changing LED lights, which can work well during certain songs. I use them at the end of practice with songs like "Over the Rainbow." Mary Lynne and others have brought several fun props to the attention of our core *Dancing Mindfulness* group over the years, including ribbons, dancing fan scarves, stress balls, and octobands.

Dancing Mindfulness facilitator Jacqueline Glaros, a former competitive dancer, also enjoys using props in her class. It is not uncommon for her to have scarves, ribbons, and noisemaking devices laid out in a corner of the room during her classes. She explains in her orientation that these props are there for people to pick up and use at any time during their practice, as long as they are mindful about whether or not their use of the props would be distracting to others.

In "Dances with Scarves" I provide some guidance on how to use scarves in your group practices.

Try This: Dances with Scarves

For this dance you will need to have enough scarves or pieces of scrap material to serve your whole group. At an appropriate transition in the practice, bring the scarves to the center of your space, making a pile. Guide participants as follows:

- Take a look at this great pile of color we have in our space.

- Now, rhythmically make your way toward a color or pattern that's grabbing your attention and pick it up. Once you've got a scarf that will work for you, just take it and toss it around in your hands for a little while. Notice its weight. If it feels inviting to you, begin moving with the scarf.

- Maybe the scarf is an extension of you. Perhaps the scarf represents a quality you wish to dance with, such as acceptance or trust. Maybe the scarf represents a piece of clothing that a character you wish to play would wear. Notice what is true for you, and in this dance, go with it.

You can modify the "Dances with Scarves" exercise in myriad ways. Sometimes I have people return their scarves to the center pile, move back out into the space, and then come back in to pick another scarf. Thus, if people didn't get their first choice of scarf, they have another chance. At other times, I have a participant keep his or her scarf until the end of practice. You can also make modifications for your personal practice as needed. When I first began exploring working scarves into my personal practice, I pulled out my entire collection of scarves and scrap material. It felt as if I were playing dress-up again, as I did as a little girl. Making this connection immediately took me to a place of beginner's mind. I began to move and to make discoveries from this renewed perspective.

Another practice that we developed in groups, "Dance the Stress Away," can be modified for personal practice as well. Credit for this dance goes to my close collaborator, *Dancing Mindfulness* facilitator and social worker Kelsey Evans. Kelsey came up with the version using a classic stress ball prop, and I modified it by conceptualizing the same idea without a stress ball. "Dance the Stress Away" can work in either group or personal practice.

Try This: Dance the Stress Away

The purpose of this dance is to consider whatever it is you're holding onto: anger, resentment, hatred—it's your choice what you want to work with.

- Take two stress balls and grip them tightly in your hands. As the music inspires you, move through the space and notice the experience of holding on.

Note

Allow time for this process. Choice of music is very important here since the "angstier" the vibe you can create, the more tension it can generate in your dancers. That is actually the point, as you will see in the next directive.

- Once the song ends, release the stress balls. Notice them leave your hands and plop to the floor.

- Take a moment to just notice how good it feels to let go of all that. Let the earth absorb any negativity that just got kicked up in the room.

A Cautionary Note

It is generally a good idea to choose the next song as a counterpoint, one that continues to work with the power of release. Also, we've learned that not everyone likes this dance. We've received some strong feedback from even regular practitioners about how too much emotion can get kicked up in this dance. In a group, all that negativity may prove bothersome. Thus, if you are going to attempt this facilitation, reissue a reminder about opting out before proceeding with this dance. As a variation, you can do the same dance without stress balls—simply have people clench their fists and when you invite the release, have them notice how good it feels to release the grip on the hands. Encourage the opening of the hands to trickle into the rest of the body and then dance with that sense of release. Although I think that just the right prop can help you to tell the story of your heart, mind, and soul, I try to avoid making the scarves or other props the focus of the practice. In many classes, I don't even use them or I offer them merely as options.

Sharing and Witnessing

Since practitioners in *Dancing Mindfulness* classes move with each other, they generally witness each other's stories. There are two facilitation strategies you can employ to invite more direct witnessing among participants. Often, I invite participants to come into a big circle, usually during a high-powered song that inspires busting out of the dance moves. Then I open the circle up, asking one person at a time to come in and do a solo. This is similar to the Runway Dance (page 57). I usually step in first and take the lead to model. You can also do this same exercise by inviting practitioners to form groups of four or six, depending on the size of your class. Encourage each person in the group to take a turn, although participants can always opt out.

A deeply connective dance can happen when class members pair off in twos. One person goes first to dance their story while the other witnesses the story, and then the partners change places. This pairing and alternate witnessing approach is a time-honored form of shadow work in many conscious dance and movement therapy traditions. Depending on the length of the song, you, as the facilitator, can rotate who leads and who witnesses. Such dances are powerful; however, it may feel awkward or not optimally safe to casual dancers coming for a class. My best suggestion is to use this dance only with a group of people who are used to dancing with each other. In personal practice, you have the option of sharing your dance with a trusted confidant. You might also consider using an exercise like the dance and poetry fusion offered below, adapted for a group setting.

Try This: Group Dance and Poetry Fusion— A Retreat or Study Group Activity

This exercise is similar to combining dance and poetry or another creative channel covered in the previous chapter. However, in this activity we will take that similar spirit into a group.

- Have the members of your retreat or group dance along a certain theme: the example I use here is "finding God in our dance."

- After the dance, invite each of the participants to write one or two lines about their experience with the theme.

- You, as the facilitator, or a group member can work to combine them in some way to make a cohesive poem. This poem offers a story of that group's experience during that particular practice.

- Sending group members away with a final copy of the poem offers a lovely memento of the experience. In the example used here, we elicited responses in an online forum. Thus, if you are facilitating a distance-based group or forum, this activity can be used as a call to creative contemplation.

Finding God in Our Dance
By the Community of Dancing Mindfulness Facilitators

In the subtle movements in the flow of dance, I meet the God of my understanding. With each organic movement, born of genuine response to music or silence, the spirit speaks through my body.

God is with me when I am dancing—divine souls, lost in sweet music, which heals like golden honey when I am hungry.

God is the Original Dance, the one already turning within me when I allow myself to yield to it and join in.

Dance reveals in me an ecstatic and passionate connection to Spirit. It is the greatest love affair of my life. As I surrender to the dance of breath and movement, the whirling, twirling, collapsing, and reaching, this is the place where I meet the Divine. And ultimately myself. Coming to believe we are one and the same.

Dance is my best Soul practice, where body, soul, god, and community meet and align.

Dance releases me from the world and allows me to just be. God moves my spirit to laugh, cry, and let go of my fears.

Dance circumvents the mind, allowing the spirit to commune as one with its creator. Dance is the reflection of that communion!

Dance releases the glow of the spirit within my soul, body, and mind. It's not a reflection of what's within. It's being within myself and allowing the release of the divine touch of God, allowing my spirit to flow freely without judgment. Truly being in the moment of a free-floating spirit.

Dance brings me back to my body, back to my heartbeat, my breath, back to communion with the eternal Now.

There is a moment in the dance when troubles fade, when my mind is clear and I find my place. I spin to the center and

I move inside, to where I find myself and I lose my pride. He meets me there and I see His face, He dances with me in that open space.

Flowing totally with the essence that is sometimes visceral, sometimes unexpected. Where the rhythm of my soul meets and gives BIRTH to Oneness though Movement. Dance is born ... and I express The Divine in me in Motion. And so it is.

To find him is to feel enraged and to feel alive, to experience sorrow and tranquility, helpless with one step, and empowered with another, to twirl, to leap, no longer invisible. The greatest gift he bestowed on us was the ability to heal ourselves through the art of dance.

God is everywhere, but he hangs out even closer to me when we dance.

Contributors

Jamie Marich, Mindi Berg Thompson, Christine Valters Paintner, Chris Campbell, Shelly Heilweil, Jane Peachey, Yemaja Jubilee, Kirsten Koenig, Vicki England Patton, Fonda Kingsley, Marta Mrotek, Sasha Webster

Weaving It All Together

I am deeply moved by how dancing mindfulness practitioners use media such as poetry, painting, drawing, and filmmaking as modes of expression. *Dancing Mindfulness* facilitator Marjolein (Maddy) Zijdel, originally from the Netherlands, now living in New Jersey, uses short filmmaking as a vehicle for embracing the stories of her journey. She composed a short film, called *A Song for the Unknown*, during a difficult time in her life as she met serious roadblocks in her training to be a professional dancer. Although I recommend watching the video if the technology is available to you, you can still witness the transformation as she shares some of her story in print form:

I have been dancing my whole life. It was my whole world and I didn't know any better. So, when I went to college, it made sense that I was going to major in it. Halfway through college, my passion for dance started wilting and my heart began to feel emptier and emptier. I didn't want that passion to die out, but making my passion a career wasn't as wonderful as I thought it would be. I got injured and had to continue dancing through the pain. After that I got depressed. Being told I wasn't dancing well enough and being graded for something that was supposed to be an interpretation of my soul just took its toll. I didn't want to do it anymore. I was halfway through school so I didn't want to quit. I didn't want to turn back, so I pushed through, crawling broken to the finish line. I was a real mess during my senior year, but with the right help, I was able to graduate, cum laude, at the end of the year.

Many scholars cite an enhanced ability to describe emotions and experiences with words as a fruit of mindfulness practice. However, the pain of traumatic experiences can literally render people speechless—unable to access the part of their brains that can express such deep pain verbally. For Maddy, the power of creativity intervened to help her process her emotions when words could not. Before she even met me or became acquainted with the formal *Dancing Mindfulness* practice, she was using creative mindfulness as a way to sit with and then move through burdensome emotions. Now she is able to look back and use words to describe what happened, and she has also been able to rewrite the ending to her story. As Maddy explains:

The help I received from different social workers was tremendous. I was inspired. I wanted to do the same thing. I applied to the graduate school of social work on a whim. The July after I graduated, I found out I was accepted. I started that September and have found a new passion, a new love, a new career. After discovering all of this, I also rediscovered my passion for dance through dancing mindfulness. I learned how much of an outlet dancing can be for my emotions and for others' emotions, so when I found out about the *Dancing Mindfulness* facilitator certification, I jumped at the chance to complete the course. It was a beautiful experience and I am so honored to have participated in it. My *Dancing Mindfulness* work was also immediately put to use in my campus counseling agency where I completed my internship. Ever year, my agency holds an event called "The 24-hour Truce." We plan twenty-four hours of programming to promote a world without violence. During one twenty-four-hour event, I held two *Dancing Mindfulness* sessions. The theme for the first session was "a world with and without violence." I had about ten participants and they all participated fully and enjoyed their time. I asked them to paint the room with their bodies, showing and portraying what violence looks like. Then I had them wash it all off, cleansing the walls, their bodies, and their souls.

Maddy's story is a testament to the power of embracing one's brokenness and transforming that brokenness into something lovely and renewed. Taking it a step further, Maddy was then able to share with others this dynamic practice of telling the story, embracing it, and transforming it. In my experience, dancing mindfulness practice allows for this process or can provide a powerful adjunct to other healing practices. You may not yet feel that you can share your story publicly or share the practice with others, and you certainly don't have to. Begin by honoring where you are at today.

I draw inspiration from the words of West African poet Ben Okri: "Stories can conquer fear, you know. They can make the heart bigger." When I consider the power of story in those terms, how can I not jump right in and dance my story? My healing and my continued transformation depend on it.

Try This: Story, the Seven Attitudes, and the
            Creative Arts

My healing and transformation depend on me dancing my
story.

I can embrace it using all modes of expression that are available to me and all elements of dancing mindfulness.

What is keeping me from dancing my story today?

• Consider the seven foundational attitudes of mindfulness
  practice: nonjudging, patience, beginner's mind, trust, nonstriving, acceptance, letting go.

• How does each attitude relate to story? Consider taking each
  attitude and dancing a story to go along with it.

• How can working with your story help you to further develop
  these seven attitudes for your optimal health and well-being?

I encourage you to use dance, or any of the other creative arts, to
contemplate these questions—get out your journal, your paints,
your pencils, your camera—whatever helps you enter this place
of contemplation. Perhaps you are a songwriter, a poet, or a fiction writer. Consider these channels to help you dance with the
questions. Notice the connections that rise up when you fuse the
practice of dancing mindfulness together with any of your other
practices or creative pursuits.

Other Voices on Story

Brown, Brené. *Daring Greatly: How the Courage to Be Vulnerable Transforms the Way We Live, Love, Parent, and Lead*.
New York: Avery, 2015.

Gottschall, Jonathan. *The Storytelling Animal: How Stories
Make Us Human*. Chicago: Mariner Books, 2013.

McFarlane, Marilyn. *Sacred Stories: Wisdom from World Religions*. New York: Aladdin, 2012.

White, Michael, and David Epston. *Narrative Means to Therapeutic Ends*. New York: W.W. Norton & Company, 1990.

Video Resource

- "A Song for the Unknown" by Marjolein (Maddy) Zijdel. Available at www.dancingmindfulness.com/resources.

Chapter 7

Fusion

Resting in Wholeness

Life is the dancer and you are the dance.

—*Eckhart Tolle*

In graduate education, aspiring helping professionals learn about the various approaches to psychotherapy and theories of psychology. During my own graduate study, certain aspects of each theory resonated with me, but I found that one single approach was insufficient to frame my work as a helper. It delighted me to hear about the eclectic approach to counseling, in which professionals draw on a variety of models to inform their practice. While for some more conventional professionals *eclectic* translates as "having no direction," being an eclectic immediately resonated with me, especially because my worldview is something of a collage.

As my professional and personal development proceeded, *eclectic* didn't seem like quite the right word. Several years ago I settled on *integrated* as a better word to describe my approach to life and learning. *Integration* comes from the Latin word *integrates*, the fusion of incomplete parts into a whole. It comes from the same root as *integrity*, or wholeness. As the folk saying goes, the whole is more than just the sum of its parts. An experience in dancing mindfulness is more than just the body, more than just the breath, more than just the story you may tell with your dance. An experience in dancing mindfulness is the convergence of many elements, resulting in wholeness so much greater than any one of these things. Whether you choose to call this element integration or fusion, we recognize that the magic is in the convergence of all elements.

The Pursuit of Wholeness

Sacred teachings in various traditions emphasize the importance of pursuing wholeness. When I consider my own reasons for engaging in spiritual practice, a primary motivation is to achieve this sense of wholeness, unity, and integration—not only unity with my sense of the Divine, but unity with humankind, with nature, with time, and with the cosmic convergence that fuses it all together. For instance, a modern translation of the Zhuangzi, a collection of Chinese stories and fables that are central to the Daoist path, offers this wisdom:

> Life, death, preservation, loss, failure, success, poverty, riches, worthiness, unworthiness, slander, fame, hunger, thirst, cold, heat—these are the alternations of the world, the workings of fate. Day and night they change place before us, and wisdom cannot spy out their source. Therefore, they should not be enough to destroy your harmony; they should not be allowed to enter the storehouse of the spirit. If you can harmonize and delight in them, master them and never be at a loss for joy; if you can do this day and night without break and make it be spring with everything, mingling with all and creating the moment within your own mind—this is what I call being whole in power.[1]

Like many friends and colleagues who are spiritually sustained by the fusion of Eastern and Judeo-Christian spiritual teachings, I consider

Thomas Merton a trailblazer, and not just because he published a version of the *Zhuangzi* for a Western audience. Merton's commitment to interfaith understanding and the spiritual fruits it yields epitomizes the beauty of fusion as a spiritual concept. Merton writes in his classic *No Man Is an Island*:

> There is something in the depths of our being that hungers for wholeness and finality. Because we are made for eternal life, we are made for an act that gathers up all the powers and capacities of our being and offers them simultaneously and forever to God. The blind spiritual instinct that tells us obscurely that our own lives have a particular importance and purpose, and which urges us to find our vocation, seeks in doing so to bring us to a decision that will dedicate our lives irrevocably to their true purpose.[2]

There is connection between the sense of wholeness we can discover in spiritual practice and realizing the fullness of our life's purpose and mission. I've experienced this phenomenon for myself with great joy since formally deepening my dancing mindfulness practice and I am delighted to witness it in others who dance with me as well. Modern mindfulness teacher and scholar Dr. Tara Brach offers a salient explanation for how this experience unfolds: "On this sacred path of Radical Acceptance, rather than striving for perfection, we discover how to love ourselves into wholeness."[3]

One tale that I love above all others distills the essence of fusion for me, especially as it relates to dance and wholeness. I first encountered this tale in studying Hasidic folklore at an earlier point in my journey. I'm grateful to my friend and fellow *Dancing Mindfulness* facilitator Ramona for once again bringing it to my attention. The story is retold in several modern sources, although I am especially delighted that Lawrence LeShan tells it as such in a book called *How to Meditate*:

> There is the Hasidic tale of the great Rabbi who was coming to visit a small town in Russia. It was a very great event for

the Jews in the town and each thought long and hard about what questions they would ask the wise man. When he finally arrived, all were gathered in the largest available room and each was deeply concerned with the questions they had for him. The Rabbi came into the room and felt the great tension in it. For a time he said nothing and then began to hum softly a Hasidic tune. Presently all there were humming with him. He then began to sing the song and soon all were singing with him. Then he began to dance and soon all present were caught up in the dance with him. After a time all were deeply involved in the dance, all fully committed to it, all just dancing and nothing else. In this way, each one became whole with himself, each healed the splits within himself which kept him from understanding. After the dance went on for a time, the Rabbi gradually slowed it to a stop, looked at the group, and said, "I trust that I have answered all your questions."[4]

As you continue to delve into your personal practice, paying more attention to the element of fusion, consider drawing inspiration from this tale. How can your dance allow you to become whole with yourself, healing the "splits" and the wounds that keep you from living the life that you deserve?

Setting Sail with Personal Practice

At several points in this book, I've made suggestions for how you can combine two elements together in your dancing mindfulness practice. Allowing for the convergence of two or more elements is a major way to work with the element of fusion. Such moments of fusion support us in our movement toward wholeness. For instance, consider allowing your breath to match your body movement, allowing your body to tell the story of your heart, and letting your sense of the Divine that dwells in your spirit work out the roadblocks to progress in your mind. Anytime you bring together two or more elements, you create fusion at its most basic level. At a more complex, inexplicable level,

fusion is what emerges in your practice when you realize a completeness that can only be achieved through this beautiful convergence. In
other words, the *Aha!* experience.

Whenever a vital shift occurs in our mind that allows us to see the
world with new insight, we experience such moments. Some are life-
changing. Others are significant, although not necessarily monumen-
tal. As a therapist, I've learned that change happens in our lives when
we allow the flow of these *Aha!* connections to become part of our
experience and we are open to what they teach. Maybe, in response
to such a moment, you've said something along these lines: "It just
clicked" or "All of a sudden it made sense." These shifts can happen
during many processes, like therapy, prayer, or a conversation with a
good friend. As both a therapist and a *Dancing Mindfulness* facilitator,
I've seen these shifts occur most potently when they involve a fusion
of the body, mind, and spirit elements.

The personal journey of Melita Travis Johnson, an African-American
clinical social worker from Grand Rapids, Michigan, exemplifies fusion
of the elements and attitudes of dancing mindfulness, and her witness
moves me. Melita dances with a commanding presence, with every
note of the music, her eyes and face tell a powerful story. Just before I
danced with her for the first time, Melita was coming out of a toxically
injurious situation. She recalls:

> I walked into my first *Dancing Mindfulness* experience racially
> and culturally bruised and wounded. After forty years of stellar
> work performance—without cause—my job was threatened and
> my workday was insidiously traumatized by a ruthless, tyran-
> nical, white female CEO/owner. I had planned a phased retire-
> ment. Instead, I made a healthy choice to leave the menacing
> noxiousness that had characterized my workplace. Two weeks
> later, I entered the *Dancing Mindfulness* space. I was wound so
> tightly I could feel nothing but anger, hurt, and resentment. I
> kept the commitment to attend because, at my core, I under-
> stood and believed that *Dancing Mindfulness* could be a highly

useful treatment component for survivors of trauma, specifically black women. I left my thirty years of clinical practice, impassioned to reach out to one of the most high-need, underserved populations in society—overwhelmed black women, like me.

When I arrived, I realized just how shielded I had become in the presence of white women. As I observed the room they exclusively populated, I was initially and instinctively taken back to that poisonous place of annoyance and guardedness. The women were cordial. In fact, as I further explored the group and looked beyond their race to their humanity, I looked into the faces of a group of women who looked like I felt—cautiously needy and seeking. As I quietly sat in contemplation, I reflected on who I am and what I was bringing to this experience and I reviewed the reality: my black ancestors have mindfully, spiritually, and bodily danced through tribal rituals, middle passages, barbaric enslavement, Jim Crow laws and enforcement, lynchings, white race riots, beatings, dog bites, water hoses, torched homes and churches, stolen and murdered children, and numerous other legalized forms of degradation and inhumane segregation. Talk about the fusion of breath, body, soul, spirit, and sound into the story of dance, and you're talking about the history of my black enslaved foreparents in America....

Focusing on my ancestors and dance led me to realize that my people and I have a clear legacy of transcending physical, psychological, and environmental circumstances by dancing. This reaffirmed my opinion that many black women who might be offended by the notion of a therapy group, or alienated by engaging in the practice of yoga or other mindfulness interventions, might comfortably embrace *Dancing Mindfulness*.

Being raised in the black community where almost everyone danced and most danced very well, I always viewed my ability as mediocre, at best. I always loved music and would always dance with abandon in the privacy of my bedroom with my mirror-partner. But, here I was, dancing with ten other women in an expansive mirrored room. I was tentatively nervous, overly self-conscious, and intensively striving to do it right.

Then I breathed.

I realized—with an almost-audible sigh of relief—everyone in the room seemed to be far more concerned with their own journey than they were with mine. They were moving in their own space, and experiencing this moment in their very own way. With this realization, I started letting go, trusting and connecting with my own body. Creating my own story in my own way. Nobody was looking at me. Everybody was dancing. For the first time in my life, I just settled into the moment. I came out of my "head" and allowed my body to move with the sounds and the music. I didn't have to worry about whether I was dancing right or wrong. I just danced. I stopped thinking about my fifteen months of workplace inequity or my people's five hundred years of racial oppression.

I just danced.

Finding Fusion in Rest

There are multiple ways to foster fusion in dancing mindfulness. Although the movement we cultivate during our dances can stimulate these convergences, much of it truly crystallizes during the moments of stillness and rest. Rest is just as vital as movement in dancing mindfulness. Blogger Maria Popova, whose forte is writing about the brain and creative processes, observes:

> The best ideas come to us when we stop actively trying to coax the muse into manifesting and let the fragments of experience float around our unconscious mind in order to click into new combinations. Without this essential stage of unconscious processing, the entire flow of the creative process is broken.[5]

It's little wonder that many in the modern-day conscious dance movement highly regard Popova's work! Another blogger, Adam Ericksen, puts even more of a spiritual twist on the convergence of rest, wholeness, and discovering one's true purpose. He reflects:

> Rest is important because the human heart is restless until it rests in the love of God. When our hearts are restless we are run by the expectations of others, of our culture, that says our value is based on doing.... Until we find time to rest and remember the radical love of God, we will seek to find love, admiration, success, or approval in all the wrong ways.[6]

When you practice dancing mindfulness on your own, it is very important for you to give yourself a period of rest (*sivasana*), just as you would in a yoga or *Dancing Mindfulness* class, to conclude your formal practice on any given day. When you allow yourself this period of rest or stillness, notice which elements of your practice emerge as the most meaningful. Or, you may notice nothing at all. The most important component to focus on is the "sinking in" of your experience.

If you like guided meditations and struggle with meditating (in a traditional sense) or settling down on your own, this time of rest offers an opportunity for you to practice. Perhaps you struggle with just *being*. I suggest that you go through the other six elements of dancing mindfulness to guide your period of rest. For instance, you can scan these elements by focusing as follows:

- My breath—I honor my breath. What am I noticing about my breath?

- My heartbeat—I honor my heartbeat. What am I noticing about my heartbeat?

- My body—I honor my body. What am I noticing about my body?

- My mind—I honor my mind. What is on my mind? Can I allow it to quiet?

- My spirit—I honor my spirit. What is happening in my spirit?

- My story—I honor my story. What have I discovered about my story today?

- And I come back to my breath. May I always come back to my breath.

I prefer the terms *rest* or *stillness* instead of *relaxation* because many people I practice with set themselves up for self-judgment when they feel they can't relax. They set themselves up for frustration in a final meditation exercise by striving—by setting a goal of total relaxation. *Relaxation* is a loaded word because it is different for everyone. Moreover, your experience in the final meditation may simply come in the form of *just being* or identifying a greater sense of stillness in the mind. You may or may not be relaxed when you do this, and that's okay. Nonstriving is the attitude of mindfulness that I would encourage you to consider if you fear, somehow, that you are failing because you can't relax. If you identify with what you're reading in this paragraph, you're in good company! You don't "win" at mindfulness or any meditative practice if you can sit or lie down in perfect stillness for long periods. The fruits of the practice manifest when you can draw your attention back to the present moment, when you become aware of the wandering. Mindfulness is the journey home to the present moment, and ultimately to your authentic self.

Try This: Guided Rest (*Sivasana*) Meditation

If you know that coming into your own rest period never seems to work as well as when someone is leading it in a class, consider recording your own voice reading this script on your cell phone or another recording device. When you come to the end of your personal practice, simply press PLAY. If hearing your own voice bothers you, go to an online source like YouTube. There you'll find plenty of guided meditations (see "Other Voices on Fusion," on page 147).

- Come into a position that feels comfortable for you, something that you can maintain for minutes at a time. Most people like to lie down, although you are free to modify. Allow your body to settle in and feel the connection of your body to the earth, to the ground below you. Give yourself some time to go through this process.

- If you like, think about the beauty of the earth supporting you. Consider the heavens above you giving you comfort, like a blanket. Notice the healing power of the energy surrounding you, enveloping you from all directions. With every breath, allow your body to settle deeper and deeper into its space. Allow some time for this settling to take place.

- Thank your body. Thank your body for showing up to the practice today. Perhaps you took some risks today that you were not expecting to take. Thank your body for taking those risks. Thank your body for showing up for you, especially if your tendency is to judge it harshly. Practice acceptance of your whole body, of your whole self. Thank your body for helping you tell your stories today, the stories of your life, the stories of your spirit.

- As you notice your body settle more deeply into the space, allow your mind to quiet, allow your spirit to experience grace and bliss. For the next few moments, you have nothing to do, you have nowhere to go. Your only task is to *be*. Just listen to the music in our space and allow what you hear to connect with your breath—your vital life source—the place where we began, and the place to which we will return.

During any rest meditation, it is wise to work with music that is ethereal and contains no lyrics. There are plenty of choices for this, especially if you have a collection of yoga CDs or music for meditation. Experiment with what works for you in your individual practice to help your body settle. My general pattern is to pick one song that does not have lyrics yet evokes that feeling of unwinding. Then, I end practice with a short (two- to three-minute) song that uses lyrics yet still maintains a mellow vibe created in the space. I generally choose a song with lyrics that are very meaningful, and I use similar songs for group practices. Pieces like Snatam Kaur's "Long Time Sun," Loreena McKennitt's "Dante's Prayer," and the various covers of the Beatles classic "Blackbird" work very well. I'd love to hear which songs are your favorites as you practice! (See Resources for Dancing Mindfulness, page 185, for ideas on connecting with our community.)

Launching Out: Sharing the Practice with Others and Deepening Your Personal Practice

Several practitioners of dancing mindfulness are in recovery from an addiction or a mental health issue like depression, anxiety, or post-traumatic stress disorder. When people talk about the role that dancing mindfulness plays in helping them to achieve a greater sense of wellness in their recovery journeys, I beam from ear to ear, realizing what fusion means in a broader sense. Demi Jacobs, first a student in a *Dancing Mindfulness* community class and now a brilliant facilitator in her own right, is one such person. On the role of dancing mindfulness in allowing her to experience a greater sense of wholeness, Demi reflects:

> I love dancing! It revealed that I had been holding onto parts of me, stages of life that I thought I had forgiven myself for already. It revealed a frightened child within who needed permission to move on. It was so beautiful to have that weight lifted.

Recovery transformed Demi, and the dancing mindfulness practice entered her life at a crucial point in her recovery journey. She recalls:

> When I attended my first dancing mindfulness class, I was at a stage of my recovery where I was learning more about a god

that is personal to me. I never really believed in a traditional conception of God, but due to mainstream belief systems I found myself feeling guilty for not believing what I had been "taught" to believe, which kept me from much of a connection at all. I was sensitive, unsure, fearful, and I had all of this emotional baggage that I was sorting through and didn't know what to do with.

When my recovery sponsor told me about this class, I was elated. It was like it clicked. I've always loved to dance, and yoga and meditation had sparked an interest, although at that time I had no experience with either of them formally. So we went. And I fell in love. I can remember the excitement of dancing to different genres of music that I hadn't heard before, challenging myself to follow the suggestions offered, allowing myself to just be me. Not judging. Not striving. Just being. Through that, it hit me that I found a higher power, in the present moment. One of love and tolerance, who could not be defined but had been waiting for me to just slow down and let him in.

Demi's story affirms that recovery can be about more than just getting clean; it's truly about the sense of wholeness that the process of holistic recovery can cultivate. If you believe that there is no hope for incarcerated addicts who've hit such a low bottom as a result of their drug and alcohol addiction, you simply have to meet Demi and take one of her classes. They are some of the most graceful, spirit-filled journeys in conscious dance I have experienced. The light she is able to share with our community is proportional to the darkness that she experienced in her active addiction.

If you, like Demi, are experiencing the call to share your personal practice with a group, consider that all the ideas shared to this point in the chapter can be woven into group facilitation. I make it a point to end all my group practices with the "Guided Rest (*Sivasana*)" meditation that I already shared. Although *lying there* is a big part of what this pose is about—resting in the bliss of doing nothing—*sivasana* is not wasted time. It is the most important part of the practice because that is where the fruits of the practice come together in a kind of wholeness. Interestingly, this is challenging for many, especially those who struggle with anxiety and have a problem sitting still. Just as with other parts of yoga or dancing mindfulness, it must be practiced.

During one particular facilitation experience, I recall a regular dancer in one of my classes lying next to me in the studio during this final rest period. She had a difficult time keeping still. One of the most vibrant women on the dance floor, she actively engages in the vigorous parts of practice. Yet she turned to me and sheepishly said, "I can't do this. I can't relax." I advised her to be gentle with herself, to notice what was coming up in her body without judgment and then direct some breath to that area. All elements of dancing mindfulness give you opportunities to practice and learn new things about yourself. This dancer learned that she needed to practice the art of resting. As a facilitator, I considered it a privilege to hold space for her and to support her in this process.

Weaving It All Together

The art of wholeness and the art of rest are both explored in this chapter. I share ideas for working with the element of fusion. Although the most obvious expression of fusion may be the extended rest experience at the end of a practice, every time you allow two or more elements to blend in your practice you're experiencing fusion. The blessed unfolding of these fusion experiences can set a path forward filled with connections and convergences that we need as we cultivate a sense of wholeness.

I am once again drawn to a story of another dancing mindfulness practitioner and facilitator as I contemplate the power of fusion. These ideas I present about healing and wholeness may help you as you develop your personal practice. Speaking for myself, ideas best come to life when I behold how they play out in a real-life story. Chris Campbell's lived experience encapsulates the beauty of both informal dancing mindfulness personal practice and the joy of finding a *Dancing Mindfulness* class. Her story exemplifies the element of fusion. Chris explains:

> I discovered dancing mindfulness at the age of five. It was a common day. I was invited over by some older teenage girls to come play "American Bandstand" in their makeshift playhouse, an abandoned school bus carcass discarded at the end of their driveway. I can remember it like it was yesterday when the 45rpm began whirling on the little plastic record player and they encouraged me to "strut my tiny stuff" down the aisle of the bus to the thumping sound of "These Boots Are Made for Walking." Without knowing it, I embodied my first element of dancing mindfulness: breath. As I was given permission to show up fully in a nonjudging environment I felt myself inhale fully and exhale completely.
>
> Unbeknownst to me I had been holding my breath since birth, as if to guard myself from harm. As they smiled and cheered me on, I remember, for the first time ever, I felt joy well up inside of me until it overflowed to the point that I had tears pouring out of my eyes. My face had spent many of my short five years covered in tears but never from joy. I couldn't contain this new feeling nor did I want to. I felt a foreign sense of freedom and of letting go as I danced, shimmied, swayed, and, of course, strutted. This dance brought me intense elation, a lightness of Spirit. For the first time ever, I wasn't trying to be good enough, smart enough, perfect enough. In fact, I wasn't striving at all. I just was. I was one with my body, my breath, the amazing sounds. I caught myself giggling like the other girls I would enviously watch on the playground at school, and I didn't even know why I was laughing. I do now. I had touched my innocence.
>
> I must say that I didn't have much to laugh about at that time. I was growing up in a home ransacked by alcoholism. I grew up in the tender yet tumultuous sixties and seventies with

a lot of family secrets. By age eleven I began discovering sub-stances that would bring me fleeting feelings "similar" to that of the abandoned bus dances and the safety of the hedgerow bliss I had enjoyed. That discovery caused over twenty years of self-destruction, including full-blown alcoholism by the time I was fourteen. I eventually found sobriety through a 12-step program, although my return to movement didn't come for another forty-six years.

A friend in casual conversation mentioned going to a *Dancing Mindfulness* class. Something on the visceral level sparked. Instantly following her suggestion, I went online and unfortunately found there wasn't a class anywhere near me, but I immediately ordered the DVD. Well, let's just say I haven't missed a day of movement since. I began taking dancing mindfulness breaks each hour at work—a perk of the less-than-stellar-fitting job was a solo office where I could close the door and dance. I would close my office door and "drop in." I found my breath again. My spirit. A new story began to emerge. At the end of those sanity breaks, I felt like I could go on. These mini–dancing mindfulness moments gave me the energy and clarity and con-nectedness to my mind, body, and spirit that I needed. When I got home at night I would dance as best I could for twenty min-utes. On days when I didn't have to go into work early, I would start my day dancing.

As I began training deeply on my own, I found myself sud-denly devastated by a mysterious back injury. In the first days following the injury, I missed dancing more than anything as I lay on the floor day after day. Some days all I could do was focus on the rhythm of the dance of my breath or do my best to embody the vibration of sound. In my mind, I would tell a new story by visualizing my cells moving inside my body, heal-ing the inflammation, pushing the bulging discs back in place, soothing the angry muscles in my hips. I would mindfully move one leg, then the other. I would gently arch my back to a crescendo of music. During this challenge I had no choice but to practice acceptance and nonstriving. As soon as I could stand upright, I tapped into the element of beginner's mind and began to mindfully stand for five minutes, ten minutes, as long as I could and sway, listening carefully to my body's needs. I was literally teaching myself to listen to my inner wisdom and trust that my body, with its now weakened spine and damaged hip structure, would support me in a new and glorious way. I learned unique ways of moving and I embraced this meditative form of movement like a hungry child with a fresh orange. I devoured every drop of soul nectar available. Daily I practiced nonjudging as I fell short of my ego's goal to return to full movement each day.

Slowly, dance by dance, moment by moment, as all the elements and attitudes fused together, I not only found physical health but my spirit healed in miraculous ways. I have danced in *witness* each morning as the fifty-three-year-old woman I am has organically merged with the enchanted five-year-old school bus queen of the strut. Twelve weeks postinjury I regained full range of physical motion from my daily practice and much more importantly I have regained full range of motion in my heart.[7]

Your journey with dancing mindfulness will be distinct from Chris's because you come to this practice with your own story. We honor and celebrate that in dancing mindfulness. Chris was able to weave the attitudes and elements of her story together, making space for a sense of childlike wholeness to return. Consider how having a regular, creative practice like dancing mindfulness can revive, revitalize, and restore. How might it help you bring the various pieces of your experience together? The words of one of the favorite authors of my youth, Madeleine L'Engle, illuminate how this process manifests for me in dancing mindfulness: "The discipline of creation, be it to paint, compose, write, is an effort towards wholeness."[8] Of course, I augment her list slightly to include the dance.

Try This: Fusion, the Seven Attitudes, and the Creative Arts

My dance allows me to rest in wholeness.

How does my dance allow me to bring together the various pieces of my life experience?

What connections do I experience between wholeness and rest?

- Consider the seven foundational attitudes of mindfulness practice: nonjudging, patience, beginner's mind, trust, non-striving, acceptance, letting go.

- How does each attitude relate to fusion? Consider taking each attitude and dancing with it using two or more of the elements. Alternatively, you can bring up each element as a focal point for your final rest meditation (*sivasana*) over your next several personal practice experiences.

- How can working with fusion help you to further develop these seven attitudes for your optimal health and well-being?

I encourage you to use dance, or any of the other creative arts, to contemplate these questions—get out your journal, your paints, your pencils, your camera—whatever helps you enter this place of contemplation. Perhaps you are a songwriter, a poet, or a fiction writer. Consider these channels to help you dance with the questions. Notice the connections that rise up when you fuse the practice of dancing mindfulness together with any of your other practices or creative pursuits.

Other Voices on Fusion

Csikszentmihalyi, Mihaly. *Flow: The Psychology of Optimal Experience.* New York: HarperPerennial, 1990.

Greenough, Millie. *Oasis in the Overwhelm: 60-Second Strategies for Balance in a Busy World*, 2nd ed. Charlotte, NC: Beaver Hill Press, 2012.

LeShan, Lawrence. *How to Meditate: A Guide to Self-Discovery*. New York: Little, Brown, and Company, 1999.

Naparstek, Belleruth R. *Invisible Heroes: Survivors of Trauma and How They Heal*. New York: Bantam Books, 2004.

Multimedia Resource

• HealthJouneys.com (Belleruth Naparstek's official website with numerous guided visualization recordings and resources).

Chapter 8

Leading by Example

Fostering Healing Experiences and Creating Community

Great artists are people who find the way to be themselves in their art. Any sort of pretension induces mediocrity in art and life alike.

—*Margot Fonteyn*

Karlene (Kar) Rantamaki embodies dancing mindfulness. Born with cerebral palsy, she never let that get in the way of claiming her birthright to dance. Kar is a vital member of our *Dancing Mindfulness* tribe in the Youngstown-Warren, Ohio, area, where I am based. Rarely does a Thursday go by when Kar does not show up to our space, ready to practice dancing mindfulness, even if she has to do it from a chair or using the assistance of her crutches. She recalls,

"When I first started mindful dancing, I felt like a leaf blown off a tree swirling in all different directions. I was timid, scared, and did not know what to think. There was a part me that felt I was being judged. Over time and with constant practice I am realizing that I hold myself to higher expectation of achievement and I am judging myself."

Kar dances with such an organic sense of both joy and tenacity that reminds me why I love this practice so much. In discussing her experiences with mindful dancing, Kar points to the importance of dancing in community: "This form of dance says there is no judgment on anyone who steps into the collective swirling energy of this community."

Among its many attributes, *Dancing Mindfulness* allows for the creation of strong communities that support the healing process. This chapter offers you some ideas for structuring practices to build and best serve community practice. As both a student and a teacher, I know that many people out there learn best if they have a structured flow to follow, at least at first, before doing their own thing. In this chapter, I explain what constitutes a class in *Dancing Mindfulness*. There are two major areas that I need to cover in order to achieve this mission. The first area is commitment to safety and flexibility in designing your classes based on context within a three-phase model. In trauma work we call the stages of this three-tier model:

1. Stabilization
2. Reprocessing
3. Reintegration

In simpler terms, classes must have a beginning, a middle, and an end. You wouldn't push participants into deep, heavy emotional work without first warming them up and easing them into the practice. You wouldn't conduct this type of emotional work in a class without first going over some guidelines with them on how to keep themselves safe during the practice, which, of course, includes options for sitting out certain dances.

The second area to cover is the definition of leadership as it applies to facilitating *Dancing Mindfulness* community practice.

Safety within a Three-Phase Model

As a clinician who primarily specializes in the treatment of traumatic stress issues, safety is my gospel. Without the commitment to keeping a client safe, and fostering this safety throughout our therapeutic relationship, I run the risk of causing my clients harm as well as destroying the foundation on which to build our therapeutic process. The primary way in which I see both clinicians and wellness professionals—yoga teachers, dance instructors, life coaches, bodyworkers, healers—jeopardize safety is by pushing people too far too fast. Another major way to threaten safety is by not properly preparing a person for what to expect, which often goes hand in hand with not returning to a neutral, safe place at the end of a session or class.

I am certainly no saint in the area of safety, and I am constantly striving to learn more ways to keep my clients safe through the unexpected terrains of psychotherapeutic explorations. A common saying suggests that experts learn everything they know by making mistakes, and I've certainly made my share. For instance, when I was a young therapist leading a client through some breathwork, I invited her, out of habit, to close her eyes and follow my lead. She seemed uneasy throughout the entire exercise. Relaxing in the dark, she later told me, brought up painful emotions for her. It makes sense, considering that the horrible sexual abuse she endured as a child happened in the dark. I apologized and tried to repair this breach in trust as best that I could, but ultimately the client never returned. I am indebted to her for the invaluable lesson she taught me.

Whether you are a mental health/addiction professional, a wellness professional, or a member of the community experiencing the call to facilitate others in dance, know that there are small measures you can take to create an environment of safety.

A Culture of Choice

Fostering choice at every juncture is a powerful way to create a safe space. Inspired by the lesson I learned from my former client, I never tell people to close their eyes; I always give clients and students the option. I may say something like, "I invite you to close your eyes if you're comfortable doing that" or "You can do this with your eyes closed or open, whatever feels best for you." When leading *Dancing Mindfulness* classes, I let participants know that they can opt out of doing any dance or song, or any movement that I may suggest. Although I ask participants to be respectful of other dancers if they need to sit out a dance or leave early due to discomfort, I strive to empower them with choice. You may be surprised by how much the offer of choice makes people feel at ease. Traumatic life experiences can take away our sense of choice and empowerment, and we can help people reverse the script by practicing these simple measures.

Avoid Forcing Intimacy

I once heard a popular conscious dance form criticized by a trauma survivor as having too much "forced intimacy" with other participants. Although I was not at the particular class to evaluate the statement for myself, I relate to it, as I have been in conscious dance classes where such forced intimacy is an apt descriptor. I also experienced suggestions for movements, especially in groups, that made me feel uncomfortable, and I didn't receive any kind of message from the facilitator that I could say no. Although I am not opposed to groupings in certain songs within *Dancing Mindfulness*, forced intimacy ought to be avoided to promote safety within the practice.

Establish Safety Guidelines Early

The facilitator's opening statement is a crucial component of a group *Dancing Mindfulness* practice. This statement sets the tone for a physically and emotionally safe practice. I believe it is important to address the following points in your opening statement (these are similar to those established for personal practice at the beginning of the book):

- **Footwear.** On a hardwood floor, I generally advise people to go barefoot. Some people may feel more comfortable to start with their socks. However, I advise them to proceed with caution if they still want to keep their socks on when they come into standing movement; socks can be slippery. Of course, dance shoes of any kind—basic ballet slippers, jazz shoes—generally work on hardwood surfaces. On carpet or other surfaces, the footwear issue is generally not a major consideration. You want your participants to be comfortable yet mindful of their safety in movement. Even when I teach on carpeted surfaces, I still make the statement about footwear being the participant's choice. It's a small way to communicate, from the very beginning, that you are concerned with their well-being, and it sets a safe tone for the practice.

- **A Brief Orientation to Mindfulness.** This is an opening statement, not a lecture, so refrain from giving a long discourse on mindfulness. Communicating some version of a definition will suffice. However you introduce the concept, participants must know that mindfulness is simply about noticing experience without judgment and honoring what comes up. I let my participants know that there isn't a right or a wrong way to do this class, as long as they are being mindful of their experience. In my view, setting a mindful tone from the first few moments of the class is paramount in keeping the practice safe because it keeps people from pushing themselves.

- **Honor Your Limits.** Invite participants to listen to their bodies throughout the practice and avoid pushing themselves further than the body can safely go. Even if you are teaching at a studio or in a program where signing activity releases is common practice, there is no greater safeguard than hearing a facilitator make a comment about physical limitations at the beginning of the practice. Some variation of the statement "Listen to the body" is in order. Although listening to the body is a skill that we practice in the first few moments of a *Dancing Mindfulness* class, for the sake of safety, it is worth mentioning in the opening statement. I usually tell my participants that while the practice may inspire them to push harder, especially when they see others engaged in dance, listening to when the body says "too much" is vital in avoiding injury. Putting your concern out there generally helps to set a safe climate.

- **Opting Out Is Always an Option.** Let your participants know that they don't have to dance every dance, and they don't even have to engage in every movement, step, or grouping. A person's belief that he has a choice is the very essence of empowerment. If he needs to leave the dance space to get a drink of water, take a moment to rest or reflect, or simply sit on the sidelines to hold space for the other dancers and witness their movement, I ask that he be respectful of other dancers who are still in the practice.

- **Emotional Safety.** Letting people know that opting out is an option is one of the best ways to help set an emotionally safe tone for the practice. Another way is to let people know that sometimes dance can be an emotional experience, and to assure them that you will be available at the end of a session if they need one-on-one process time. Of course, only say that if you intend to make yourself available. I strongly suggest that you do. Many teachers fear that saying this will open up the floodgates of all these people who want to spill at the end of a session but, believe it or not, an opposite effect tends to occur. Just knowing that you're there if something comes up is a simple assurance that keeps many feeling safe.

Many would-be facilitators have fears about the potential for participants to experience intense emotional responses during *Dancing Mindfulness* practice. An acquaintance of mine who is trained in another conscious dance form told me, "It's like we opened up all of this stuff and people started crying and breaking down and I didn't know what to do with it." In any type of conscious dance practice with an emotional focus, people are likely to experience deep emotions, perhaps manifesting as tears. Such openings are not always negative; catharsis can be healing. A well-crafted opening statement that alerts people to your availability when the formal class is over serves as an excellent preventive measure to breakdowns that breach safety. It reinforces the supportive environment. During practice, when I see someone having a deep emotional moment, I usually make an effort to dance near her as a way of seeing if she needs extra support; sometimes a simple hand gesture or making eye contact sends a powerful message, like "I'm here for you." However, it is not usually feasible to stop a class to attend to the needs of one person. Of course, in extreme circumstances, which are rare but may still occur, if your inner senses tell you a person is feeling so unsafe you need to do something, my best suggestion is to let the music keep playing. Hopefully, another experienced participant will be able to take over while you address the emergency, but if this is not feasible, trust the process and go with the flow. You'd be surprised how much facilitating the music can do on its own.

Both physical and emotional emergencies are rare, but they can happen. In my therapy practice, I embrace the "ounce of prevention is worth a pound of cure" philosophy. This means that if I take care to properly stabilize a client and make sure I don't push him further or faster than he's ready to go, I've avoided a great many potential problems. The opening statement is a major way to achieve this preemptive goal, which includes setting that tone of mindfulness for the practice. Guiding participants to listen to the subtle inner cues can help lessen the tendency to push. If in the verbal components of your facilitation you maintain the tone of mindfulness, you continue to create a climate for safe practice.

Get to Know Participants

Wherever possible, screening potential participants can be beneficial. For example, if a person in the community reaches out to you, inquires about the class, and discloses emotional problems or a mental health history, give that person a full disclosure about the class and the risks versus the benefits of participating. Ask if the potential participant works with a therapist or another helping professional. If so, you may suggest that he consult with his therapist to see if participating in such a class would be a good idea. If you are asked to facilitate a *Dancing Mindfulness* class in a clinical venue such as a mental health hospital, an addiction treatment center, or a correctional institute with a clinical component, and you're not a mental health professional, I strongly advise you to ask for a member of the clinical staff to be present during the class or available shortly afterward for any debriefing and stabilizing that may be needed.

Connect in Your Closing

The closing of a practice is also an important juncture at which to maintain the climate of safety. However you choose to end the class, be it with a final chant, prayer, or meditation, be sure to establish gentle eye contact with each participant. Bowing *namaste*, if you choose, is a good time to make this connection. If someone doesn't make eye contact with you or you sense that she is off in another world, make sure that you have some type of one-on-one contact with her before you leave to find out what the practice was like for her. Take time to assess if there is anything you need to do to help her feel stable before leaving. Sometimes she may request something as simple as this: "Can I stay in the space and meditate a little longer?" I often suggest a visit to the restroom to splash cold or hot water on the face as a bit of a back-to-the-present awakening. I reiterate my availability in the closing as well. After we formally end the practice, I don't like to give a long speech, but I remind people that I am there. A line I often use is this: "I realize that you took risks coming here today and taking part in an emotional dance experience. I don't want anyone to leave feeling that you're unsafe or threatened in any way."

Don't fret if you're not able to create a perfectly safe experience; no human being can. Inevitably, you will have participants who will not like something you do or who experience an intense emotional response. The important points I want to emphasize are that you are making the effort to set the tone for safe practice and that you are an ambassador of safety.

Flexibility within the Three-Phase Model

A significant component of safety is whether or not you are able to step into your participants' shoes. Remember what it was like when you started a new practice that really challenged you to take a risk? Think back to how vulnerable that made you feel. Unless you are facilitating in a long-standing group of the same people who are used to *Dancing Mindfulness*, there will inevitably be people in your classes who feel vulnerable. Thus you may have all kinds of great ideas about what you think a *Dancing Mindfulness* practice ought to be, but it may not be what your participants need. This is where the virtue of flexibility is paramount.

Pay Attention to the Flow and Go with It

Yogis and dancers are used to being physically flexible—or at least striving to be more flexible—but have you ever stopped to consider whether or not, as a facilitator, you are flexible? Are you able to go with the flow? For instance, you might come with a prepared playlist and a bunch of great ideas for your class. Are you willing to switch up the plan if, in reading the subtle cues given to you by your participants, you discover that your direction is not in tune with their needs? If you are expecting twenty-five people in your class and only two show up, would you be willing to modify your playlist or at least your approach to each song on the playlist? Let's say you have an active *Dancing Mindfulness* community full of experienced practitioners and, out of the blue, a few newcomers turn up who share with you, before the class starts, how scared they are to do this. How do you handle that? Although changing your playlist and plans may not be required, are you willing to modify your language to more introductory phrasing?

These questions help you evaluate where you stand on flexibility. Being flexible may sometimes prove harder with a class than one-on-one because everyone comes to a given class with different needs or from different life experiences. As with safety, there is no way to be perfectly flexible, yet I think at least having the willingness and the spirit to be flexible and meet your classes where they are is half the battle. When I train therapists, I speak often to the virtue of flexibility. Many times therapists have set ideas on how things should go in session, based on particular models or paradigms. However, there is nothing neat about addressing trauma, pain, and the experience of being human. It is important to meet people where they are on their journey and focus on cultivating their ultimate vehicle to healing. To accomplish this task you may have to deviate from your favorite model, or be willing to be eclectic and draw on the best elements of several different models or approaches. I love the eclectic spirit, and such a worldview meshes well with *Dancing Mindfulness* facilitation.

Solid trauma therapy depends on safety and flexibility; I've taught this idea to therapists for years. In *Dancing Mindfulness*, safety and flexibility are tremendously important, too, even if you are not a professional clinician.

Apply Your Personality, Style, and Strengths

As mentioned earlier, *Dancing Mindfulness* classes have a beginning, a middle, and an end. Beyond that structure I allow facilitators I train and certify a great deal of freedom in how they structure individual classes, based on their own style and personal strengths. For instance, if you are interested in working with chakras, your class may incorporate more exercises that directly work with chakra openings. If you want to take your class to a shamanic place inspired by your knowledge in that area, you certainly can. If you are working with young people and you feel that song selections need to be more contemporary, those choices are more than acceptable. Kelsey Evans, a *Dancing Mindfulness* facilitator I trained who now works closely with me, has a background in Latin dance workouts. She often creates Latin-inspired *Dancing Mindfulness* classes, and we've even joined forces to offer "fusion" classes in Zumba fitness and *Dancing Mindfulness*. The *Dancing Mindfulness* class structure is flexible, so feel free to infuse your personality, strengths, and choices into the dance practice.

As long as you warm people up at the beginning, take them to some type of deeper, exploratory place in the middle (how deep you go is completely up to you), and bring them down at the end not only to cool down physically but also to settle emotionally, the direction is yours. However, in order to keep *Dancing Mindfulness* rooted in the foundations of mindful awareness, I suggest that you address in your classes each of the seven elements—breath, sound, body, mind, spirit, story, and fusion.

Let me share an example of how I carry one of the elements—breath—through the entire practice. I start my classes and my personal practice with a few minutes of mindful breathwork in silence. Breath is my foundation. I let my participants know how important the breath is to mindful practice, and that no matter what we're doing throughout the dance, they can always come back and check in on the breath. The breath and the heartbeat will always give you good information about how you are doing and what you need in any given moment. So we may be a half-hour into the practice, working on an intense dance that is focused on storytelling, and I may call out to my participants, "Remember to keep breathing. Always come back to the breath." At the end of classes, when my participants engage in relaxation, I also issue the invitation to check back in with the breath. For me, this is where the practice comes full circle.

Try This: Revisiting the Seven Elements

Take a few moments to revisit the list of the seven elements on page xvi and consider how they may all work together in a single class experience. Think about your own style, your personal mission for wanting to lead a *Dancing Mindfulness* experience, or your intention for practicing dancing mindfulness on your own. How might these seven elements be worked into what you would like to do with your facilitation? Spend some time considering that question before moving on with the rest of your reading.

Cultivating Community Through Mindful Dance

The implications for practicing dancing mindfulness in community are many. The attitudes and elements of mindfulness, combined with some suggestions on safety and flexibility, will hopefully help as you build community. My experiences with community *Dancing Mindfulness* originated with getting a class going at my home yoga studio. This original quest evolved into taking *Dancing Mindfulness* classes into venues like health fairs and to academic/professional conferences as a way to get my peers up, moving, and considering the richness of intentional movement in the healing process.

Facilitators I train constantly bring me new ideas for building community. A group of women from Great Falls, Montana, mostly clinical professionals, took the facilitator training and returned to their hometown inspired to dive into *Dancing Mindfulness* as a self-care practice. At least once a week, usually over their lunch hour, they gather at a small local dance studio and dance mindfully. I am impressed with how these ladies came to take a facilitator training with me and then went back to their community to build a weekly gathering designed to enrich their own health and wellness as professionals. A member of this group, Shelly Heilweil, reflects, "Our practice is vital to my well-being. Period. It's the best self-care in the world. Mindful dancing, even just once a week with the group, keeps me safe, keeps me happy."

Marta Mrotek, a yoga teacher based in Phoenix, blends her *Dancing Mindfulness* training into the work she does bringing yoga and wellness practices to the recovery community. Marta notes:

> Taking the time to move more freely and feel without any expectation has added a new dimension of personal expression and creativity to my spiritual journey. This is something that I have taken into many of the workshops and classes that I teach. As a *Dancing Mindfulness* facilitator and a full-time yoga teacher, I have found opportunities to incorporate the two with ease. Movement without specific instruction provides an incredible outlet

for releasing emotion, for creating energy and letting go more completely. Whether used in a fusion class or as a stand-alone practice, *Dancing Mindfulness* is a powerful meditation tool and an easily accessible approach for connecting with healing energy.

What Makes for Dynamic Dancing Mindfulness Leadership?

Perhaps reading this book is inspiring you to bring dancing mindfulness, in one form or another, to a group or a community to which you belong. The attitudes and elements, combined with mindful movement, may offer an activity for spiritual connection if you are part of a spiritual group or ministry of some kind. Maybe you even see dancing mindfulness as suitable for a party or a celebratory setting. But how do you know that facilitation is the right role for you?

In the formal *Dancing Mindfulness* practice, the ideal facilitating leader stays true to her authentic self while inspiring dynamic movement within a safe setting that she creates. Just as we are all dancers, we are all leaders—even if we have never thought of ourselves as the leader type—if we have the ability to be genuine and inspire others with our genuineness.

An extroverted, charismatic person is not necessarily the most effective facilitator. While our culture tends to revere such types as leaders, several experiences in my time practicing yoga and conscious dance have shown me that that stereotype is often false. In my very first conscious dance facilitator training, I met some fellow trainees who, upon first impression, struck me as mousy. I'm not proud to admit that I made such a judgment. This thought went through my head: "I can barely hear these women when they speak! How are they going to get up with a microphone in front of a whole class and lead a class in a *dynamic* way?" Wow, was I proven wrong ...

In this first training experience, my fellow training mates displayed a variety of leadership styles. I was greatly moved by these women I initially judged to be meek. In fact, I felt an even greater connection to the dance practice by listening to this gentle, soft-spoken style of leadership, compared to the louder, more extroverted women I viewed as dynamic. Initially, I thought this preference stemmed from a balancing effect: because I am an outspoken extrovert, I am naturally drawn to people who have calmer energy. While I still believe there is some truth to that explanation, I think the major reason I experienced this attraction is the purity and genuineness with which these women facilitated. To me, the genuineness of expression is what attracts people, whether you are an introvert or an extrovert, loud or soft, big or small.

My friend and *Dancing Mindfulness* affiliate trainer Ramona Skriiko is such a powerful facilitator—and she is one of the most introverted people I know. I relish taking her classes because of the serenity and quiet confidence that she brings to her facilitation. Hearing Ramona's opening statement and breath sequence is like balm to my soul, and this balm sets the tone for practices that are transforming. As I tweaked the facilitator training intensive program, I asked Ramona to share some of her wisdom with me about what it is like, as an introvert, to facilitate a dance practice. She points out:

> During your opening statements, when introducing the concept of mindfulness and discussing safety issues, you might want to add a statement to let your dancers know that you will not be as directive as they may be used to or expecting. I usually say something like this: "I will guide you through some stretches at the beginning and let you know when it's time to get to your feet or come back to the floor. Sometimes I will make suggestions of things you might want to try. A lot of the time, I will simply be quiet and let the music guide you. Please know that any suggestions I make are optional; if they don't feel right for you, feel free to do your own thing. Just remember to be respectful of the other dancers in the room."

Ramona also highlights the importance of playing to your strengths and taking some extra time to prepare. She adds, "Remember to extend the attitudes of nonjudgment, acceptance, and patience to yourself! You don't have to be perfect to be a good facilitator. You just have to be genuine."

In my counseling practice, I've worked primarily with alcoholics and addicts deeply affected by trauma. The people I work with can spot a phony a mile away. If I meet my clients with the most compassionate version of my genuine self, there is a greater chance we'll forge a solid therapeutic alliance. Being genuine can include admitting when I might not have all the answers and when I'm stumped by a certain situation a client brings to the table. Being genuine can also mean that, if appropriate to the client and the setting, I often let my snarky sense of humor peek through. While ethical behavior that does no harm to the client is paramount, I maintain that being the most compassionate version of your genuine self sets you up for success.

Teacher versus Facilitator

When I decided to offer *Dancing Mindfulness* facilitator trainings, I purposely selected the word *facilitator* instead of *teacher*. *Teacher* implies an expert-learner or mentor-protégé relationship. Dance teachers, by definition, provide technical and choreographic instructions. Quite often, hard-driving methods of the notoriously rigid kind are a reason that many dancers abandon their love of dance. I do not intend to insult professional dance teachers. My own dance teachers over the years taught me a great deal about the craft of dance, and I regard many of them as highly compassionate, loving souls. I simply wish to make a distinction—a facilitator implies a relationship of equality. At the root of the word *facilitation* is the Latin word *facile*, meaning "easy." Thus, it is the job of a facilitator to make the path—in this case, the path of mindful exploration—easier than if someone were pursuing it alone.

It takes a great deal of humility to embrace the facilitator's mind-set, and I feel this mind-set is what distinguishes *Dancing Mindfulness* from many other conscious dance forms. Seeing yourself as a gentle, encouraging guide is essential to the style of *Dancing Mindfulness* facilitation and leadership that I envision. As I've explained throughout this book, valuing the physical and emotional safety of participants is a prime component of conscious dance facilitation. Being flexible, which is a trauma-sensitive value, is another key component of *Dancing Mindfulness* leadership. It takes a solid leader to step back from his agenda for the good of the group. While we may associate qualities like charisma and dynamism with well-known leaders throughout history, I would argue that the willingness to adapt for the good of the group trumps charisma any day. High-energy extroverts and calm, even-keeled introverts can be equally excellent *Dancing Mindfulness* facilitators if they commit to safety, flexibility, humility, and genuineness.

The concept of the "authentic self" gets good buzz in the fields of psychology and self-help, almost to the point where its become a cliché. I prefer the term *genuineness*. Person-centered or humanistic therapy, associated with Dr. Carl Rogers, posits that the core values of empathy, unconditional positive regard, and congruence are vital to successful work in therapy. In the Rogerian approach, congruence and genuineness are synonymous. Genuineness, in the context of leadership, is your ability to offer others the best version of yourself. Don't get me wrong: sometimes in the energy of a full class, when the music is pumping, I can put on a little more of a character or get more energetic than usual—maybe even lose some of my inhibitions in a positive way because the practice elicits this work. These experiences are to be expected when you are facilitating *Dancing Mindfulness*. Just don't cross the line into being phony. Facilitation is not acting. Rather, it is guidance toward a meaningful, transformative practice for those along the path.

Your capacity for genuineness as a *Dancing Mindfulness* facilitator is directly proportional to your willingness to practice what you preach. If you have a regular mindfulness practice through dance or any other channel, you will automatically be a more effective facilitator than someone who does not. For this reason, I recommend regular, personal practice in dancing mindfulness and other practices like yoga and more traditional, seated meditation if you wish to facilitate

Dancing Mindfulness. There's an age-old saying in the psychotherapeutic professions that you cannot take a client further than you, as the therapist, have gone yourself with your own work. In Christian Scripture, this verse from Luke (22:26) impressed me, even as a young child: "The greatest among you must become like the youngest, and the leader like the servant." These pieces of guidance, which inspired my formation, encapsulate the beauty of beginner's mind.

Am I Ready to Facilitate *Dancing Mindfulness*?

The following are qualities that can be used to describe an effective *Dancing Mindfulness* facilitator. If you want to take your self-discovery a step further, you may consider meditating or free-verse journaling on each quality and, in the spirit of curiosity, see what is revealed. An effective *Dancing Mindfulness* facilitator:

- Commits to the safety of participants.

- Possesses a "go with the flow" attitude (that is, flexibility in action).

- Practices genuineness.

- Regularly engages in mindfulness practices.

- Has a deep desire to share the benefits of mindfulness with others.

- Honors the dignity of all people coming to a class.

- Recognizes that beauty comes in all shapes and sizes.

- Appreciates the dancer in everyone.

Facilitating Mind-Body-Spirit Connections

We open our weekend *Dancing Mindfulness* facilitator trainings to anyone who has a background as a helping professional (for example, psychotherapists, social workers, psychologists), yoga or other fitness teachers, and educators. I prefer that people who go through formal facilitator trainings have some type of experience working with people, yet even this qualification is more of a guideline. I am willing to make exceptions if a person can demonstrate the call she is experiencing to lead others in mindfulness practice, although I may require some additional one-on-one work, depending on the situation. Above all, my desire is for facilitators to have the qualities described in "Am I Ready to Facilitate *Dancing Mindfulness*?" on page 165, and these may or may not be embodied by working professionals.

For Jessica Tupa, a professional dancer and clinical counselor, taking the weekend facilitator training elicited several key insights about her role as a teacher and helping professional in general. Jessica notes:

> Though I have used a mindfulness outlook (based mainly in Buddhist practice) for myself for many years, the main premises of mindfulness as Mindfulness were not entirely clear for me. And I did not necessarily have a starting place at which I could meet my clients. Here's the important part: I realized that the *Dancing Mindfulness* weekend training clarified this for me so that I could make mindfulness a part of my outlook, vocabulary, physicality, and experience. The training gave me extra and new tools to help integrate the mind-body training I already had.

It warms my heart that a team of collaborators active in *Dancing Mindfulness* practice (both as formal classes and as a way of life) offer facilitator trainings. Irene Rodriguez, a native of Puerto Rico currently based in Florida, is the first facilitator to offer her own trainings after continuing her study with me. Irene's passion for the practice never fails to renew my enthusiasm about what we can offer:

> This has been a beautiful journey where by moving out of my comfort zone I have become more comfortable with myself. I am learning to accept myself and love my body as it is. I feel more confident as a therapist since I have been learning how to be

mindful in the therapeutic space. I am accepting my weakness and letting go of the *I should*. This is just a beginning. Creating the playlist, promoting safety, and modeling the principles have been easy. I need to continue improving how to describe the movements and be more direct when giving instructions. I see myself facilitating and training others on *Dancing Mindfulness* as part of my career. This opportunity has allowed me to express the artist, the dancer, and the teacher that live in me.

Best Practices for Facilitating *Dancing Mindfulness* in a Group Setting

A few best practices on what makes an effective *Dancing Mindfulness* facilitator are summed up in the following points:

- Keep people safe and do not force them to explore areas they are not ready to explore physically or emotionally. Keep this as your guiding principle and you'll succeed in any setting!

- A little common sense goes a long way. Adjust both your language and your class structure accordingly. For instance, if you are facilitating a Christian-themed *Dancing Mindfulness* class, yoga language may not be optimal. If you are facilitating a group of senior citizens, tone down the physical level of the dancing, compared to how you would lead a group of teenagers, although the senior citizens may surprise you—go with the flow! That's a prime quality of a good facilitator.

- Seek help. For instance, if you are asked to facilitate a *Dancing Mindfulness* class for teenagers and your knowledge of popular music is limited, consult with someone who can tell you what will grab the kids' attention.

- Ask yourself, "What is the aim of this class?" People or organizations who book you to teach *Dancing Mindfulness* classes tend to be very clear about what they want you to accomplish (for example, a cancer survivor support group wants you to facilitate a class that helps survivors better recognize their own empowerment; a women's wellness group books you to facilitate a dance about stress relief in daily life). Having a clear purpose will make it easier for you to properly structure and facilitate the class.

- If you're facilitating *Dancing Mindfulness* in a clinical setting, the safety dynamic becomes even more important. Once again, specifying a clear purpose for the class is helpful. If you're facilitating to promote stress relief for participants who are still pretty "raw" in terms of recovery, you should keep the heavy catharsis elements to a minimum. If a group shows you over time that they are well stabilized, go deeper at your discretion. If you are a nonclinical *Dancing Mindfulness* facilitator, consult with clinical staff for their opinion on what the group can handle.

- Take class size into account. For instance, you may have a group of thirty to fifty people. High-energy, connecting dances work very well with this class size. However, you likely would find the same music a little overwhelming in a class of three to five people. Take the temperature of the room and be prepared to modify your playlist.

- If you are working with the same group consistently (say, a church or study group, a treatment center), be willing to incorporate requests in terms of music and what the group may want to address in their practice.

- Make your facilitation instructions suggestions only, and let your participants know that there is never pressure to keep up.

- How you say things and the tone you use in saying them may be more important than what you actually say.

- You do not need to talk constantly to be a solid facilitator. People won't have room to make things their own if you are always talking.

- Just because someone is dynamic does not automatically make her a good facilitator. Your genuine self always yields the best facilitation.

If you are going to lead a *Dancing Mindfulness* experience without doing in-person facilitator training, I have a few additional coaching tips for you. First, gather together a group of friends or people you know well and begin there, even if it means leading a simple class in your house. I've learned that people who know you well will have a greater tendency to go with the flow and be supportive of your learning. Second, if you go on to host a *Dancing Mindfulness* experience in public, be up-front about your experience and training. If you are already a yoga teacher, a dance teacher, a conscious dance facilitator in another tradition, or a helping professional, you will likely not have to worry about anything. However, if you lack formal training in working with others, make sure that the venue booking you for the class is aware of that. If you are an active member of a church or community group or a regular student at a studio, the people in charge will let you know if they are comfortable with you facilitating or if there's anything you will need to cover with your participants. See Resources for Dancing Mindfulness on page 185 for more information about how to receive formal training as a *Dancing Mindfulness* facilitator.

Try This: Mining for Leadership Role Models

Through journaling, sitting meditation, moving meditation, or another creative arts outlet, reflect upon a positive experience that you had with being "led." This experience could involve a classroom teacher, a music or dance teacher, a boss, or a spiritual guide. Anyone is fair game. Your task is to reflect upon what was positive about your experience. What can you learn about facilitation from this person and your experience with him or her? If you want to take the reflection a step further, you can also repeat this same task with one of your negative experiences of being led and consider the lessons that can be derived from that experience.

Other Voices on Leading by Example

Emerson, David, and Elizabeth Hopper. *Overcoming Trauma with Yoga: Reclaiming Your Body*. Berkeley, CA: North Atlantic Books, 2011.

Morrison, Suzanne. *Yoga Bitch: One Woman's Quest to Conquer Skepticism, Cynicism, and Cigarettes on the Path to Enlightenment*. New York: Three Rivers Press, 2011.

Mrotek, Marta. *Miracle in Progress: A Handbook for Holistic Recovery*. Phoenix, AZ: Wellness Meetings/Create Space Independent Publishing Platform, 2014.

Ryan, Tim. *A Mindful Nation: How a Simple Practice Can Help Us Reduce Stress, Improve Performance, and Recapture the American Spirit*. Carlsbad, CA: Hay House, 2012.

Redefining Therapy

I believe that dance came from the people and that it should
be delivered back to the people.

—*Alvin Ailey*

One of the greatest joys I've experienced during my time leading
Dancing Mindfulness classes and facilitator trainings is to watch Yuliria
Figueroa dance. Yuli embodies spirit with even the simplest of movement. As a classically trained ballet dancer, she's mastered stunning
technique, even in a practice like dancing mindfulness, where achieving precision is not the objective. By professional dance standards,
Yuli's body would be described as a larger frame, a reality that almost
kept her from fully embracing her dance. Yuli explains:

> As a ballet dancer perfectionism stole the essence of my dance.
> For years, I danced seeking to please the teachers, the public,
> the mirror. It was never enough—perfect body lines, costumes,
> hairstyles, and choreography. And so I grew up believing that
> the most perfect expression of my body was the most beautiful

and the best. But it was exhausting and stressful. So I decided
not to do it anymore.

To think of a world without Yuli dancing makes me very sad. Yet for
many spirited individuals who are dancers at their core, the pressure
to be perfect robs them of what is perhaps the most natural state of
all—the dance. The quest to be perfect drives many creative people
in the performing arts, yet it is the enemy of natural creativity, genuineness, and authentic joy. One of my favorite ice dancers, Jamie Silverstein (now a yoga teacher and eating disorder recovery advocate),
describes the struggle with accuracy:

> Of course, it was easy to define myself by an external metric or
> by what I was doing! (HINT: It's easy for *a lot* of us to find defi-
> nition this way.) I even learned to define myself by comparison.
> For me, the mores of skating kept me "swimming" if you will—
> swimming from competition to competition, from should to
> should, from restriction to restriction. I just kept swimming.
> And I did this unabashedly and without ever considering an
> alternative. When you're always trying to fit yourself in a speci-
> fied box, you never stop to question: *Why is there a box?*[1]

Silverstein's words superbly encapsulate the sentiments of my journey as well, and it wasn't just about skating; it was everything: aca-
demics, striving to be the perfect daughter, the perfect performer.
Different people and pathways filled my healing journey with solu-
tions that helped me realize that perfectionism no longer served me.
These initial interventions helped me heal. However, through mindfulness practice I've been able to shed the neat boxes that people have
given me over the years and realize that the concept of the "box" no
longer works for me. Today, I create a new way of being. I live as if
guided by a malleable essence that adapts to certain situations and
stressors that life brings my way, yet this essence is unique to me, an

extension of my practice of nonjudgment, self-acceptance, and being in the moment.

Yuli Figueroa is on the same wavelength. She observes:

> I still remember that morning of dance chapel; it was during the weekend of my certification as a *Dancing Mindfulness* facilitator. I did not take a step during half of the class, but still *I did dance*. Because dancing does not mean impressive jumps or steps, it is an intention. Dancing is a vehicle of emotions and is present in every moment ... it's a lifestyle. Dancing mindfulness allows me to reconnect with my spirit, to make a stop and live the moment. It allows me to breathe and introspectively let go. Dancing mindfulness is a healing process for me. Currently, I am studying clinical psychology and I am in the middle of developing a *Dancing Mindfulness* handbook for women in Puerto Rico who are survivors of domestic violence, because everyone should have the opportunity to experience the sense of well-being and empowerment that dancing mindfulness provides. Everyone should have their own *dance*.

Dancing mindfulness practice draws many individuals with formal dance training who, in one way or another, grew frustrated with the pressure to do it perfectly. My own yoga teacher and collaborator, Mandy Hinkle, had an experience similar to Yuli's:

> I've always danced since I was three years old. But once I really started auditioning professionally I'd always get cut right away because I don't catch onto combinations quickly and I think it really had an effect on me and made me feel like I wasn't really a very good dancer. I was living in Los Angeles for a long time and it wasn't until I moved back home and started working with Jamie that I found it wonderfully freeing to just dance again for the sake of dance and movement.

Learning to Respond, Not React, to the World

Practicing mindfulness, in any form, is not about making the world go away, nor is it about giving a big middle finger to the practice of conformity and societal mores. Rather, it is about learning to adapt to whatever life may bring in a graceful way while you remain healthy. Stress is inevitable and the modern world is a challenging, often brutal place in which to live. How are you going to respond to it? Adopting the attitudes of mindfulness—nonjudging, patience, beginner's mind, trust, nonstriving, acceptance, and letting go, among others— will help you respond to stress instead of reacting to stress. Speaking for myself, I found that I don't internalize these attitudes overnight. Cultivating these attitudes takes practice, and for me, movement and dancing mindfully are major ways that I work on improving my attitudes of mindfulness.

If you are moving in the spirit of mindfulness—staying in the moment without judgment with an intention to further cultivate attitudes of mindfulness—you are practicing dancing mindfulness. There is no neat formula that I can give you for this practice. If you were looking for a formulaic, structured practice in this book and found yourself disappointed, I hope that you were still inspired by some of the ideas presented here. Bring these ideas into your personal dance practice, experiment with them, and see where they take you. Experimentation, with an attitude of curiosity, is critical as you develop a personal dancing mindfulness practice. Dancing mindfulness does not promise to be the panacea for all that's ailing you in life, and it can certainly be practiced in concert with other healing arts to help you reach total wellness. As I often share in my writing and when I speak, no one "thing" has been the absolute key for me in my healing journey. Rather, combinations of people, practices, therapies, and modalities miraculously meshed to make me a healthier person than I was at certain points in the past. With ongoing practice in healing activities, I hope that this growth and healing will continue.

Seeking Healing Through Movement

Perhaps you picked up this book simply to develop a personal practice or explore another outlet for cultivating mindful practice. I hope that you find this book a useful starting point and that you've already earmarked some space in your dwelling for putting the ideas offered here into action. You may be feeling the call to lead others in a guided practice. If you are, I ask only two things: (1) keep people safe, emotionally and physically, and (2) construct your classes to be a unique extension of yourself in a spirit of flexibility to the needs of the group. I don't want you to be robotic copies of me. Truly, there is no box in *Dancing Mindfulness*.

Formal psychotherapy has played a great role in my healing process and I respect the practice of counseling and therapy. Additionally, I am proud of what I've been able to achieve as a counselor in helping others. However, the overall direction of where my field is going does not excite me as much as the healing wonders I witness when people organically connect with their own creativity. I see many gifted professionals in the psychotherapy field stifled in their creativity and intuition by the rigid institutions that they work for or the insurance companies they fear, imposing unrealistic medical standards of care on their work. In sum, there is only so much that traditional therapy can do for people in the modern era because of the flaws in our healthcare system.

What really excites me is what's happening in healing communities across the globe. When I see people realize that healing and wellness are not synonymous with the broken systems that so many turn to in order to heal, my heart and soul smile. Look in your local community; that's where you are likely to find structures in place for mutual help and healing in the form of nonprofits, charities, and organized community groups. For me, 12-step recovery programs and yoga studios have offered vibrant communities for healing and wellness, and as I move forward with counseling, my attention is focused more strongly on these community outlets. These are where I see so much potential for the healing power of community. In outlets like these I envision a welcome home for *Dancing Mindfulness* as a formal practice or dancing mindfulness as a personal practice and a way of life.

Dance, music, community, and spiritual practice are four constructs with proven track records of healing, originating millennia before formal psychotherapy or the medical model of care. In my view, we are foolish if we choose not to access them in some way to help us heal. Dancing mindfulness practice is a way that we can tap into all four, and the flexibility of the practice makes it accessible to virtually everyone. In my wildest dreams, I envision a movement of people who are doing just that—healing through movement. By healing ourselves, we put ourselves in a uniquely wondrous place to bring healing to the world. So what are we waiting for?

Acknowledgments

Many wonderful individuals played a unique part in bringing the formal *Dancing Mindfulness* practice, and now this book, to fruition. With great honor I extend gratitude to some of these individuals. I thank all of you who participated in facilitator training intensives and who continue to come forward for formal training in *Dancing Mindfulness*. I've learned more from you than you will ever know. I must mention by name several women in our community who continue to play a special role in shaping the practice or helping me do my job better: Abbey Carter Logan, Irene Rodriguez, Fonda Kingsley, Holly Speenburgh, Lexie Rae, Ramona Skriiko, Kelsey Evans, Demi Jacobs, and Kara Mazey. The practice, for many of us, is now a way of life. A special thank-you to the facilitators and members of our larger community who've helped me realize this truth.

Dancing Mindfulness exists as it does today because of my first yoga teacher and mentor, Maureen Lauer-Gatta. Heartfelt thanks to Maureen for a single suggestion she made several years ago that allowed *Dancing Mindfulness* to blossom. I also thank the many teachers I've had a chance to study with in my travels to places like Kripalu and Esalen and other conscious centers of learning around the world. To my current yoga, meditation, and wellness teachers, Mandy Hinkle, Jennifer Neal, Jessica Sowers, Melissa Layer, and Christine Valters Paintner—thank you for helping me to embrace the moment while challenging me to move through fear, apprehension, and pain. To my reiki master Valerie Spitaler—any words I can muster are insufficient to express my gratitude for what you are teaching me about healing and the spiritual path. The idea of having only one teacher never rested well with me because, at my core, I believe we learn from each other. I credit some of my cherished teachers in the "Other Voices" lists that appear throughout the book. My inclusion of their work is a simple act of sharing what they taught me. As my brother Paul once joked, "It takes a village to spiritually direct my sister." Today I know that's not a bad thing!

In my career as a clinician and a trauma educator, I've had the privilege of working with many colleagues, mentors, and cheerleaders. As I've developed *Dancing Mindfulness* and worked on this book project, I specifically want to thank Tommy Rosen, Dr. Steve Dansiger, Dr. Andrew Dobo, Susan Pease Banitt, Leisa Mills, Beck Gee-Cohen, Rev. John Michael Thornton, Amber Stiles Bodnar, Phil McCabe, Jeff Zacharias, Dr. Paschal Baute, Mark Metz, and Khaled Tabbara. To my sisters and brothers in other conscious dance forms who offer support, I extend special, heartfelt thanks. Thank you to my editor, Emily Wichland at SkyLight Paths Publishing, for your faith in this project and for understanding the multiple applications of mindfulness and practical spirituality in daily life. Your work on this book helped me to realize this beauty even more!

To my dear friends who continue to sustain me with their love, encouragement, and challenging insights, especially Allison Bugzavich, Joe Long, and Claire Taylor: thank you. To my stepsons, Brendan and Ethan, and all my former students turned family members, blessings and gratitude for what you've all taught me about beginner's mind. And finally, to my husband, my sun and stars, David Reiter, for everything that you are and for every way that you make my work possible—thank you! I cannot even count the number of roles you've played in promoting the evolution of *Dancing Mindfulness* as a practice and, for me, as a way of life. Gratitude!

Class Planning Worksheets

Version 1 (General)

Venue: _____

Attendees/target audience: _____

Class length: _____

Purpose or theme: _____

Mindfulness attitudes or elements of focus: _____

Other notes: _____

Beginning Sequence _____

_____

_____

_____

Middle Sequence _____

_____

_____

_____

Ending to Closing Sequence _____

_____

_____

_____

Version 2 (Specific)

Venue: _____

Attendees/target audience: _____

Class length: _____

Purpose or theme: _____

Mindfulness attitudes or elements of focus: _____

Other notes: _____

Beginning Sequence

Start on the floor for stretching and breathing: _____

Continue stretching: _____

Invite participants to their feet: _____

Standing stretches/beginning movement: _____

Explore the space/movement: _____

Energy-stirring song/connecting with others: _____

Middle Sequence

Invitation to the deeper work: _____

Sequence into deeper work/release: _____

Second song (if needed): _____

Reflective song: _____

Ending to Closing Sequence

Option:

Stay reflective or bring the energy back up (one to two songs):

_____

Final song on feet: _____

Transition back to ground: _____

Final relaxation: _____

Closing Sequence/Statement

_____

_____

Notes

Introduction

1. Jon Kabat-Zinn, *Wherever You Go, There You Are* (New York: Hyperion, 2005), 4.
2. Scott R. Bishop, Mark Lau, Shauna Shapiro, et al., "Mindfulness: A Proposed Operational Definition," *Clinical Psychology: Science and Practice* 11, no. 3 (2004): 230–241.
3. Thanks to Mark Metz, editor of *Conscious Dancer* magazine, for the great working definition. When I asked Mark for this definition, his first reply was: "We joke that when you try to define it, it no longer is conscious dance." Point well taken!
4. Jon Kabat-Zinn, "Mindfulness-based Interventions in Context: Past, Present, and Future," *Clinical Psychology: Science and Practice* 10, no. 2 (2003): 144–156.
5. Rezvan Ameli, *25 Lessons in Mindfulness: Now Time for Healthy Living* (Washington, DC: American Psychological Association, 2014).
6. Shannon E. Sauer-Zavala and Tory A. Eisenlohr, "Comparing Mindfulness-based Intervention Strategies: Differential Effects of Sitting Meditation, Body Scan, and Mindful Yoga," *Mindfulness* 4, no. 4 (2013): 383–388.
7. Martine Batchelor, "Meditation and Mindfulness," in *Mindfulness: Diverse Perspectives on Its Meaning, Origins, and Applications*, eds. J. Mark G. Williams and Jon Kabat-Zinn (New York: Routledge/Taylor Francis, 2013), 157–164. For more on *dharma*, see Bhikkhu Bodhi, "What Does Mindfulness Really Mean? A Canonical Perspective," *Contemporary Buddhism* 12, no. 1 (2011): 19–39.
8. His Holiness the 14th Dalai Lama often presents this wisdom in his public teachings. This particular version of the quote is cited in John Perkins, *The Secret History of the American Empire: Economic Hitmen, Jackals, and the Truth About Global Corruption* (New York: Dutton, 2007).
9. Jon Kabat-Zinn, *Mindfulness for Beginners: Reclaiming the Present Moment and Your Life* (Boulder, CO: SoundsTrue, 2011).
10. Paschal Baute, *Resilience of a Dream Catcher: A Spiritual Memoir* (Lexington, KY: Baute Publishing/Smashwords Publishing, 2014).

Chapter 1: Breath

1. The American Lung Association, 2015; www.lung.org.
2. William Chittick, "The Circle of Life in Islamic Thought," in *Islamic Philosophy and Occidental Phenomenology on the Perennial Issue of Microcosm and Macrocosm*, ed. Anna-Teresa Tymieniecka (New York: Springer Science & Business Media, 2007), 208.

3. Kabir, *Kabir: Ecstatic Poems*, trans. Robert Bly (Boston: Beacon Press, 2004), 45.
4. George Burke, *Learn How to Meditate: Breath Meditation* (Cedar Crest, NM: Light of the Spirit Monastery), chapter 5; http://breathmeditation.org/the-taoist-tradition-of-breath-meditation (accessed July 13, 2015).
5. If you are hungry for even more inspiration about interfaith perspectives on breath meditation as spiritual practice, visit Abbott Burke's website, www.breathmeditation. org.
6. Martha Graham, *Blood Memory: An Autobiography* (New York: Doubleday, 1991), 46.
7. Gregory Maguire, *A Lion Among Men: Volume Three in the Wicked Years* (New York: Harper, 2010).

Chapter 2: Sound

1. Maya Angelou, *The Collected Autobiographies of Maya Angelou* (New York: Random House, 2004), 391.
2. Henry George Liddell and Robert Scott, *A Greek-English Lexicon*. 9th ed. (New York: Oxford University Press, 1996).
3. "Wisdom from the Circle: Native American Quotes," Native Village; www. nativevillage.org/Libraries/Quotes/Native%20American%20Quotes3.htm (accessed June 8, 2015).
4. Douglas Spotted Eagle, *Voices of Native America: Instruments and Music* (Liberty, UT: Eagle's View Publishing, 1997), 7.
5. "Music as Spiritual Practice: A Conversation," *Sh'ma: A Journal of Jewish Ideas*; http://shma.com/2014/04/music-as-spiritual-practice-a-conversation (accessed June 8, 2015).
6. Hazrat Inayat Khan, *The Sufi Message of Hazrat Inayat Khan*, vol. II (Geneva, Switzerland: Wassenaar Publications, 1962); www.spiritsound.com/khan3.html (accessed June 8, 2015).
7. Daniel J. Levitin, *This Is Your Brain on Music: The Science of a Human Obsession* (New York: Plume/Penguin, 2006), 13.

Chapter 3: Body

1. For a modern version of the Anapanasati Sutra, consult Thich Nhat Hanh, *Breathe! You Are Alive: Sutra on the Awareness of Breathing* (Berkeley, CA: Parallax Press, 2008).
2. Swami Vivekananda, in *Vivekananda, World Teacher: His Teachings on the Spiritual Unity of Humankind*, ed. Swami Adiswarananda (Woodstock, VT: SkyLight Paths, 2006), 91.
3. Nicolai Bachman, *The Path of the Yoga Sutras: A Practical Guide to the Core of Yoga* (Boulder, CO: SoundsTrue, 2011), xvi.
4. Susan Pease Banitt, *The Trauma Toolkit: Healing PTSD from the Inside Out* (Wheaton, IL: Quest Books, 2012), 79.
5. Jan Phillips, *Divining the Body: Reclaim the Holiness of Your Physical Self* (Woodstock, VT: SkyLight Paths Publishing, 2005), 23.
6. Stephanie Paulsell, *Practicing Our Faith: A Way of Life for a Searching People* (San Francisco: Jossey-Bass, 2010), 14–15.
7. Jay Michaelson, *God in Your Body: Kabbalah, Mindfulness and Embodied Practice* (Woodstock, VT: Jewish Lights Publishing, 2007), xvii.

8. For more on EMDR therapy and related interventions, see "Resources for Dancing Mindfulness," page 186.

9. For a complete guided script on this closing facilitation, see chapter 7.

10. Anthony Bourdain, *Kitchen Confidential: Adventures in the Culinary Underbelly* (New York: Ecco HarperCollins, 2007); www.goodreads.com/work/quotes/4219-kitchen-confidential-adventures-in-the-culinary-underbelly (accessed July 13, 2015).

Chapter 4: Mind

1. Christina Sarich, "The Mind vs. Brain Debate (What Is Consciousness)?" The Cuyamungue Institute; www.cuyamungueinstitute.com/articles-and-news/the-mind-vs-brain-debate-what-is-consciousness (accessed June 11, 2015).

2. For a modern reading on the Anapanasati Sutra, see Thich Nhat Hanh, *Breathe! You Are Alive: Sutra on the Awareness of Breathing* (Berkeley, CA: Parallax Press, 2008).

3. As cited in Christine Valters Paintner, *Desert Fathers and Mothers: Early Christian Wisdom Sayings Annotated & Explained* (Woodstock, VT: SkyLight Paths, 2012), 27.

4. I do my best to provide you with as user-friendly an explanation as possible on the triune brain. If, after reading this chapter, you want to learn more, I recommend Daniel Siegel, *The Mindful Brain: Reflection and Attunement in the Cultivation of Well-Being* (New York: W.W. Norton and Co., 2007).

5. This material is adapted from the landmark work of Dr. Paul MacLean, originator of the triune-brain theory. See Paul D. MacLean, *The Triune Brain in Evolution: Role in Paleocerebral Functions* (New York: Plenum Press, 1990).

6. Many translations of "The Guesthouse" in its entirety are available online. You can also consult Jalal al-Din Rumi, *The Essential Rumi*, new expanded edition, trans. Coleman Barks and John Moyne (New York: Harper One, 2004).

7. Jamie Marich and Terra Howell, "Dancing Mindfulness: A Phenomenological Investigation of the Emerging Practice," in *Explore: The Journal of Science and Healing*; http://dx.doi.org/10.1016/j.explore.2015.07.001. *Explore* is the official journal of the Institute for Noetic Sciences.

8. Aristotle, *The Metaphysics*, trans. John H. McMahon (London: Bohn, 1857), 332.

Chapter 5: Spirit

1. Miriam Maron, "The Healing Power of Sacred Dance," *Tikkun* 25, no. 2 (2010): 61.

2. Adam Jacobs, "Why We Dance"; www.aish.com/sp/k/Why_We_Dance.html (accessed June 18, 2015).

3. Cynthia Winton-Henry, *Dance—The Sacred Art: The Joy of Movement as Spiritual Practice* (Woodstock, VT: SkyLight Paths, 2009), 2.

4. Angeles Arrien, *The Four-Fold Way: Walking the Paths of the Warrior, Teacher, Healer, and Visionary* (New York: HarperCollins, 2013), 54.

5. Gabrielle Roth, "The Spiritual Power of Dance," *Huffington Post* (May 15, 2011); www.huffingtonpost.com/gabrielle-roth/spirituality-dance_b_862226.html (accessed June 18, 2015).

6. Holy Taya (www.holytaya.com) and One Love Devotional Chant (www.onelovechant.com) are independent artists I've had the privilege of encountering in my travels. As an independent musician myself, it gives me great joy to use

such pieces in my classes. Search the Web—there are many prolific, untapped wellsprings out there, especially in the realm of powerfully sincere, spiritually connective music.

7. Bonnie Horrigan, "Shamanic Healing: We Are Not Alone: Interview with Michael Harner," *Shamanism* 10, no. 1 (Spring/Summer 1997); www.shamanism.org/articles/article01.html (accessed July 13, 2015).

8. Henri Nouwen, *Turn My Mourning into Dancing* (Nashville: Thomas Nelson, 2004), 16.

Chapter 6: Story

1. Brené Brown, *Daring Greatly: How the Courage to Be Vulnerable Transforms the Way We Live, Love, Parent, and Lead* (New York: Avery, 2015).

2. Katherine Preston, "Owning Your Own Story," *Psychology Today* (January 16, 2014); www.psychologytoday.com/blog/out-it/201401/owning-your-own-story (accessed July 13, 2015).

3. Robert Altobello, *Meditation from Buddhist, Hindu, and Taoist Perspectives* (New York: Peter Lang Publishing, 2009), 116.

4. Christine Valters Paintner, *Desert Fathers and Mothers: Early Christian Wisdom Sayings Annotated & Explained* (Woodstock, VT: SkyLight Paths, 2012), 40.

Chapter 7: Fusion

1. Chuang Tzu, *The Complete Works of Chuang Tzu*, trans. Burton Watson (New York: Columbia University Press, 1968), 73–74.

2. Thomas Merton, *No Man Is an Island* (San Diego: Harvest/Harcourt, 2002), 140.

3. Tara Brach, *Radical Acceptance: Embracing Your Life with the Heart of a Buddha* (New York: Bantam Dell, 2003), 45.

4. Lawrence LeShan, *How to Meditate: A Guide to Self-Discovery* (New York: Little, Brown, 1999), 53.

5. Maria Popova, "Happy Birthday Brain Pickings: 7 Things I Learned in 7 Years of Reading, Writing, and Living"; www.brainpickings.org/2013/10/23/7-lessons-from-7-years (accessed June 28, 2015).

6. Adam Ericksen, "The Spirituality of Rest and the Economics of Love," The Raven Foundation; www.ravenfoundation.org/sermon-the-spirituality-of-rest-and-the-economics-of-love (accessed June 28, 2015).

7. To read Chris's story in its entirety, go to www.dancingmindfulness.com/blog/how-dancing-mindfulness-saved-me-guest-post-by-chris-campbell.

8. Madeleine L'Engle, *Walking on Water: Reflections on Faith and Art* (Colorado Springs: WaterBrook Press, 2001), 70.

Conclusion: Redefining Therapy

1. Jamie Silverstein, "Confessions of an Insecure Olympian," *MindBodyGreen*; www.mindbodygreen.com/0-9578/confessions-of-an-insecure-olympian.html (accessed May 17, 2013).

Resources for Dancing Mindfulness

Other Books by Jamie Marich

Creative Mindfulness: 20+ Strategies for Wellness & Recovery. Warren, OH: Mindful Ohio, 2013.

EMDR Made Simple: 4 Approaches for Using EMDR with Every Client. Eau Claire, WI: Premiere Education & Media, 2011.

Trauma Made Simple: Competencies in Assessment, Treatment, and Working with Survivors. Eau Claire, WI: PESI Publishing & Media, 2014.

Trauma and the Twelve Steps: A Complete Guide for Enhancing Recovery. Youngstown, OH: Cornersberg Media, 2012.

Mixed Media

www.dancingmindfulness.com

Our team set up a private page for readers of this book. You will need to enter this URL for the private link: www.dancingmindfulness.com/resources.html. On this page, you can access several of the audio and video links to help you as you build your own practice or develop a program for your community. We also provide some additional resources, like stretch sequences, release forms for physical activity, and information about music licensing and other logistical matters if you choose to share the practice in the community.

Dancing Mindfulness: LIVE (DVD)

Join Dancing Mindfulness creator Dr. Jamie Marich in this live practice, ideal for home workouts or to help you hone your facilitation skills in guided dance! You can order the live practice DVD directly from our team through www.dancingmindfulness.com. (You may be able to find a better deal on Amazon.com or a similar site, especially if you stream video.)

Connect with *Dancing Mindfulness* on Social Media

Consider connecting with us on social media to share your experiences and ask questions. Our most active forums for general community participation are on Facebook. We have a main "fan page" set up as Dancing Mindfulness, and a discussion group called "Dancing Mindfulness Community Forum" that you can easily search and join. Many of our facilitators and communities have several smaller pages set up, too. Spanish-speaking groups exist as well, moderated by affiliate facilitator Irene Rodriguez.

Training

Visit www.dancingmindfulness.com/training for information on Jamie's weekend retreat-style facilitator trainings. This website has the latest, most updated information for you to access about becoming a certified *Dancing Mindfulness* facilitator. Jamie gives about four trainings herself each year. Additionally, a distance-based mentorship program is available, where interested people can study with Jamie or her affiliates via web-based technology and be eligible for certification. In 2015, affiliates of the Institute for Creative Mindfulness, Jamie's continuing education company, began offering *Dancing Mindfulness* facilitator trainings in other parts of the country. Jamie also launched an advanced training track in 2015. Trainings are generally small (no more than twelve to fifteen participants), so consider booking sooner rather than later if you are interested.

Bring Jamie to Your Event

If you are interested in bringing Jamie to your facility to offer a training retreat in *Dancing Mindfulness*, send an email to info@mindfulohio.com to begin the conversation.

Liability Insurance

Many new facilitators are concerned about liability and malpractice issues involved in leading a physically dynamic practice like *Dancing Mindfulness*. If you work for a studio or a clinical facility, consult with your facility's insurance carrier to see if doing this type of work is covered by your current policy. In my experience, it usually is. If you are still unsure, there are several types of malpractice insurance for dance instructors or wellness professionals available online. You can find out which one works the best for you by doing a simple Google search. Please contact us at Mindful Ohio (info@mindfulohio.com) if you have any questions.

For More on Conscious Dance

For a comprehensive listing of most conscious dance practices, including listings about trainings and events, go to www.consciousdancer.com. This is also the current home page of the association DanceFirst.

Index of "Try This" Practices

CPSIA information can be obtained
at www.ICGtesting.com
Printed in the USA
LVHW040022190822
726311LV00004B/359